THE BRANDYWINE

THE
RIVERS OF AMERICA

Edited by
STEPHEN VINCENT BENÉT
and CARL CARMER

As Planned and Started by
CONSTANCE LINDSAY SKINNER

Art Editor
RUTH E. ANDERSON

THE BRANDYWINE

by

HENRY SEIDEL CANBY

Illustrated by
ANDREW WYETH

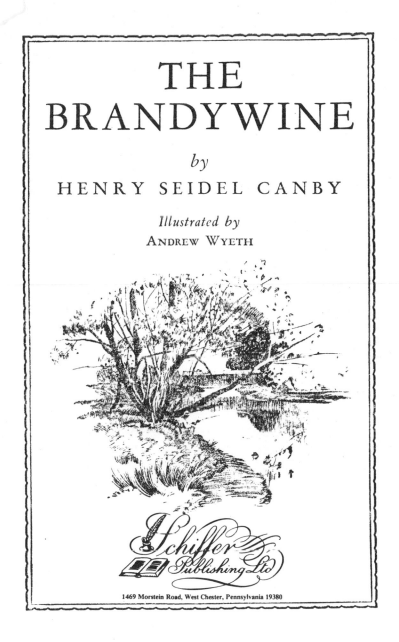

Schiffer Publishing Ltd

1469 Morstein Road, West Chester, Pennsylvania 19380

Published by Schiffer Publishing, Ltd.
1469 Morstein Road
West Chester, Pennsylvania 19380
Please write for a free catalog.
This book may be purchased from the publisher.
Please include $2.00 postage.
Try your bookstore first.

The Brandywine

ISBN: 0-916838-06-4

Printed in the United States of America.

Contents

Foreword

I HAVE a deep affection for the Brandywine, the river which is the subject of this book, and on which I was fortunate enough to be born. But there is another motive, equally impelling, which has led me to undertake its history. Watercourses have character and personality, as much so as cities and towns, and few are richer in this respect than the Brandywine. These fluvial characteristics have always been interesting to me. I have been attracted by rivers as Thoreau was attracted by swamps. Rivers and their valleys have impressed themselves upon my imagination and upon my memory; and I have seen enough of the world to become, if not a connoisseur, at least an interested student of the way in which they influence human life and are, in turn, humanized, exploited, and made part of civilizations. In all this observing, the Brandywine has been my point of departure and standard of comparison. A resident of New Haven, in Connecticut, will measure all moun-

tains—small or large—by his East and West Rocks.
So I have used the Brandywine in estimating the characteristics of rivers, from the Avon to the Mississippi.

When I travel, I notice rivers particularly, as
industrialists notice factories, educators note schools
and colleges, and novelists detect outcroppings of
human nature. And I have found that my reactions
to rivers differ as sharply as my reactions to men and
women. The Mississippi, for example, and to begin
with a heresy, seems to me, in its upper reaches at
least, to be a rather uninteresting river; whereas the
Missouri, slashing its muddy current around sharp
bends, is urgently alive. The Seine, for all its load of
history, never impressed me except as an excellent
waterway, though I have boated down miles of it;
while the upper Thames, no larger than the Brandywine, is as rich in character as a Dickens novel. The
Hudson, according to me, is one of the noblest of all
rivers. The St. Lawrence, in sense of magnitude and
powerful flow, exceeds the Father of Waters. The
most impressive river I know is unknown to fame and
has no history or culture on its banks. This is the
Skeena, a broad, full-rushing torrent, banked by
forests of great trees, sweeping under gray snow-
streaked mountains, and irresistibly carrying the
waters of British Columbia to the Pacific.

Some rivers famous in history, like the shallow

Greek streams or the canallike Guadalquivir near Seville, are commonplace to the view. Others, like the Rhone with its blue flood hastening without pause from Alps to Mediterranean, seem never to have had the final word said about their urgent beauty, in spite of libraries of description. For sheer beauty, there can be few rivals of the Oconalufty—that lucid water flowing over an opalescent bed beneath cliffs of Carolina rhododendron hung with blossoms. For violence of tumbling water, I have never seen the equal of Kings in its Sierra canyon, a rush of milky-blue waves in one constant, boiling slide and fall to the hot and dusty valley of central California. For powerful richness and exuberant fertility commend me to the Santee of South Carolina, a yellow flood licking back into forests of cypress, tupelo, and magnolia.

The Connecticut has another quality, that of making its own characteristic type of meadowed curve and valley from upmost New Hampshire to Saybrook on the Sound. The Danube, at least from Austria into Serbia, has this faculty also; more so than the Rhine, which looks as if Hollywood had made it. Such little French rivers as the Epte or the Rance represent the watercourse entirely dominated by man. They seem to have been canalized from birth. The Concord is a lazy river. The Susquehanna is a wandering river. The waterways of the Norfolk Broads are rivers skulking from the sea. Some rivers are too exotic to be humanized, such as that stream, I do not know its name, which runs, boiling hot and sulphurous, down a gorge hung with orchids and trailing rope vines to the Caribbean at Puerto Cabello in Venezuela.

I admit that the midwestern rivers of our continent do not attract me, except the Illinois streams which have quality, especially when in flood. They pass, so many of them, from the filth of industrial cities to the bucolics of corn-country mud. The famous Platte is a spillway rather than a right river; the Rio Grande is disappointing; the Colorado is lost in its canyon; the Schuylkill is paved with derelict coal; the Delaware is noble in its estuary, but an inferior Connecticut above; the James lacks only mountains to be another Hudson; the Columbia (heresy again) is magnificent but often monotonous.

There are degenerate rivers also, such as the Naugatuck in Connecticut, which has become a ditch for metal waste; or the once fine East River of New York, fine still if you do not look too closely at the fluid garbage of its waters; or those Maine dead-waters that crawl sluggishly from dam to dam through a no man's land of devastated forest.

I do not think that I include the Brandywine among the personable rivers just because I love it. It was a personable river before it began to have a human history, and has been made only more so by three centuries of dams, parks, mills, and the cultivation of its banks. Therefore I hope, in the pages that follow, not to lose sight of the strong individuality of this stream while telling the story of its geography, its economics, and the societies in its valley. After you read this book, go and see it for yourself, preferably in the first week of May or the second week of October. You will understand then why I am desirous at the beginning of this history to make clear that this river has a character of its own as well as a history.

HENRY SEIDEL CANBY

THE BRANDYWINE

CHAPTER ONE

A River's History

WHAT is the history of a river? It is surely not the same as the history of a country, or a city, or a nation, or a race. Nor is it merely a geologist's account of so much water wearing down so much rock into a valley and forming, with its sediment, so many miles of plain. Rivers are dynamic, even the quietest. They make a road and a living place for men. They give them power to use, they create trade, they invite battles, they determine, in some degree, the quality of cultures. More than any other agency of nature, they make the earth usable by man. Hence, so it seems, the history of a river should begin with an account of how the pressure of flowing water created a valley, and a description of that valley. And it should then concern itself narrowly with the river's part in the history of a human society. The Thames made London, but its history is very different from a history of London. It is one element of that history, and of English history, which is difficult, but not impossible, to separate from the rest.

The subject of this book is no Thames or Hudson. It is a little river, only about sixty miles long from its double source to its mouth, with no world capital on its banks. It is not a famous boundary river, as is the Potomac or the Rio Grande; it is not a traffic river, as is the Mississippi; it was never a lumber river like the Kennebec or the Susquehanna; it has no Grand Canyon; it does not penetrate and open a continent like the great St. Lawrence. The Brandywine, on which I was born and in whose valley my ancestors have lived for six generations, is navigable above its two-mile estuary only by a canoe, and not even a canoe, in all probability, has ever made the trip up its falls and rapids. Yet it does enter the Delaware at the exact point where the northern regions of industry and small-farm agriculture end and the plantation region of the South begins. It has a distinctive beauty, and an unusual grasp upon the imagination of those who know it well, and it has made history—military, social and economic—for three centuries. Thus it offers an excellent opportunity to study those subtle ways in which a river can influence events and men.

Indeed, the Brandywine is so small a stream, even when judged by European standards, that its historian's first task is to prove that it is a river at all! In Delaware and lower Pennsylvania it is called Brandywine Creek, and so designated on the maps. If there is a river in the state of Delaware, so it used to be said, that river is the Christina (called Christiana before the tercentenary of the Swedish settlement), into whose channel, navigable for ships of fourteen feet draft, the Brandywine flows just before the entrance into the three-mile wide estuary of the Delaware River.

Actually, the Brandywine is a perfect example of the typical small river of the eastern seaboard, differing from type—and here to the great advantage of the Brandywine—only in that its fall line, where the stream drops into the coastal plain, is at tidewater and the beginning of a ship channel only two miles from the open passageway to the Delaware and the sea. The Christina, however, whose deep dead water winds for seven miles and ends in a small stream, is a perfect example of what Swedes, Dutch, and English of the seventeenth century meant by a creek, which they pronounced, as we school children did, even when our teachers rebuked us, not *creek*, but crick. Creek, in earlier English, and in Dutch, Swedish, and French, is a word of probable Teutonic origin which signifies a winding estuary or cove—a watery shelter, usually in marshes, up which a ship could sail. Only in later American usage, and in Australia, was the name transferred to a small river or a branch of a river. The Brandywine, for its first two miles through lowlands and marshes—which was all that the Swedish settlers at their first landing saw of it—was a creek in the true sense. Above that it is a river, rushing

down 120 feet in its first four miles, with enough
water to turn a dozen great mills at the end of its
last falls, and scores of small ones above. If I call the
Brandywine a creek in this book, it will be because of
habit, not geography.

Even a tiny river, however, may have at least
three possible claims upon history: the use made of
its waters, its beauty, and the men and events whose
course was determined in some measure by its flow. In
each of these respects the Brandywine, small as it is,
proves a fortunate choice for a writer who happens,
as I do, to love it, for it has strong waterholds upon
an American reader's attention. Once famous for
spawning fish, this river, thanks to its geology, made
possible one of the greatest developments of power in
all the American colonies. Flour and gunpowder first
became great American industries on its banks, paper
in rolls was first manufactured there, and textiles
went through some of their important inventive
stages. Brandywine flour and meal were carried the
length of the seaboard and to the West Indies, fed
starving armies, and slaves on the sugar plantations.
Brandywine powder made the name of Dupont famous. The joint estuary of the Brandywine and the
Christina opening into the Delaware, created in Wilmington a trading port of cosmopolitan culture, and
for a brief period, because of revolution and persecu-

tion abroad and yellow fever in Philadelphia, centered here one of the most interesting émigré groups in the history of the United States. The Swedes and Finns, who sailed into the Brandywine in 1638 because ships could there be unloaded on a rocky shore, brought with them the knowledge of how to build a log cabin, which was to make life endurable in winter in the century-long movement of Americans through the Appalachian forests toward the west.

It is not too much to say that the Brandywine, which has been under four flags—Swedish, Dutch, English, and American, has contributed to an un-usual variety of culture. There was the Indian first— and plenty of evidence shows that for the Indians the Brandywine was a well-loved stream. There was the pioneer society of Swedish, Dutch, and English clus-tering around the estuary, and combining agriculture with trade. There was, by accident and for a little while only, an island of French culture of the old regime in a little community become suddenly cos-mopolitan. And later came the provincial but pro-gressive industrialization of a typical small city of the United States, Wilmington, to which Brandywine power and the Brandywine tidewater contributed. Early in the nineteenth century, in the secluded gorge, rich in power, above Wilmington, the du Ponts re-created a French family industry which only slowly conformed to American practices. And above them, in the rich valley of Chester County, was a Quaker community, homogeneous, prosperous from the rich grazing in Brandywine meadows, which had a life and even an architecture of its own. Still farther north on the slopes of the hills were the feudal holdings of the ironmasters, English and German, again a culture with definite qualities. And all these cultures produced men and works of widely different kinds. Nor were the habits of life and mind developed on the Brandywine local in character. When Chester County was organized, its western boundary could have been called the Mississippi. The Brandywine societies, like those of New England, spread fanwise into the west.

I shall make no attempt, for reasons stated, to write in this book the entire history of those parts of Pennsylvania and Delaware through which the Brandywine flows. I shall touch state history and national history only where the Brandywine touches them. But the Brandywine did make power, and hence industrial and economic history. With the Christina, it was responsible for a racial admixture prophetic of the forces that were to shape American culture. Its upper valley sheltered what was perhaps the most characteristic Quaker society in the country,

and was the home of aesthetic rebels against its restrictions, such as Bayard Taylor and Thomas Buchanan Read. And the river itself caused the Battle
of the Brandywine.

CHAPTER TWO

Geographical and Geological

THE Brandywine is not, strictly, one stream; it is two, plus an estuary. The Brandywine valley also, even though the land areas responsible for the river are so small, is not one valley, but several. A low range of hills, the first uproll of the Appalachians, runs from near the Susquehanna toward the Schuylkill, some thirty to sixty miles back from tidewater. These so-called Welsh Hills, named from the Welsh Quaker who settled their eastern regions, make a distinct ridge rising to a thousand feet, which, from a distance, looks like a mountain range though, close at hand, there are no impressive heights. Thus far came glacial drift, though not the great continental glacier; and the slopes of these sandstone hills, with outcroppings of trap, rough, stony, infertile, are more like Connecticut than Pennsylvania. Their crests make the northern county line of Chester County; over the ridge, the deeper valleys and higher mountains of upper Pennsylvania begin. Close together, in one place hardly a mile apart, on the southern slope of the Welsh Hills and in Chester County, are the sources of the two Brandywines, the east and the west. Mountain brooks at first, many small streams unite to form two channels, which quickly diverge

13

into a long ellipse, not to join until the Forks, about fifteen miles in an airline, much more by water, from the top of the Welsh Hills. It is the west branch that is the longer and more considerable, and is regarded as the parent Brandywine.

The two Brandywines, leaving the range, wind through lower hills, and cross, a few miles apart, the Great Valley of southeastern Pennsylvania, a limestone trough that stretches from the Schuylkill to the Susquehanna, as straight as if laid down with rulers. This is now the route of the main line of the Pennsylvania Railroad.

Below the Great Valley, the Brandywines work their way through low hills, highly cultivated for the most part, making valleys that are rich, good to look at it, good to farm on the slopes and graze on the water margins. Below the Forks, now become a sizable river, the Brandywine runs on through much the same kind of hill country until it crosses the Delaware line. Here, encountering ridges of hard granite, it cuts its way in a wild and beautiful canyon and drops at the Great Falls—so called by the pioneers— into an estuary in the marsh lands where it meets the Christina and joins the broad Delaware. Those who follow Route U.S. 13 from Philadelphia to the South cross a bridge, between Brandywine Village and Wilmington proper, which spans the Brandywine at the exact point where the tumultuous, rock-rushing stream falls into a great pool into which ships once sailed from the Delaware and the sea.

Geologists describe the Brandywines as "strong streams," flowing from the slopes of an uplifted peneplain of quartzite. The united river has an average flow of 279 cubic feet a second. These streams run through remnants of the Piedmont plateau, and cross the Great Valley transversely; indeed, they cross all strata transversely. The Great Valley itself, which has no continuing stream, seems to have been undermined by underground waters and eroded down to its present level by streams, like the Brandywines, which flow across it draining its surface water. Continuing through the so-called Baltimore gneiss and Wissahickon schist of Chester County, the Brandywine encounters above Wilmington the aforementioned range of harder igneous rock, called gabbro, the granite of Brandywine commerce. Here, at first a slow stream in a gently sloping valley, it gradually cut for itself a gorge in the granite hills, down which it rushes to tidewater. It is the soft gneiss of the middle Brandywine that makes, when weathered, the orange-shaded houses and plum-cake barns of that valley. The blue gabbro of the Wilmington hills is responsible for the rusty, darker walls of old Delaware homes. Fresh cut, it is hard and unlovely.

In the Chester County course of the Brandywine are dikes of green serpentine, unhappily used in
the ugly seventies and eighties for building, and beds
of limestone and of feldspar. On the "barrens" made
by the infertile serpentine, many rare minerals have
been found, corundum in sapphire shades and dia-
spore. In the unstratified pegmatite which, here and in
upper Delaware, contains feldspar of great purity,
are garnet, beryl, and tourmaline, which sometimes
crystallize in great perfection. In one now deserted
quarry, near a county poorhouse, and on the borders
of the Brandywine, an exquisite orthoclase feldspar
occurs in crystal forms like hovering butterflies. They
are iced with tiny stained crystals of quartz on which
are laid brilliant rods of red rutile. This was named
Chesterlite after the county of which the Brandywine
is the ruling stream.

But to return from geology to geography, the
point at which the Brandywine at its estuary enters
the great alluvial plains that spread over all the tidewater South is of peculiar interest. Here the fall line
of the river is almost on a bay of the sea—which
proved to be of high commercial importance. And
here, if an informed observer climbs the hill above
Brandywine bridge at the end of the rapids, and takes
an elevator to some high window of the Dupont office

building, he can see and study the meeting place of
two economic and social cultures.

To the north and west is the Brandywine country of hills, smallish farms, millsites, where proprietors worked for themselves. To the south and south-
west stretches the coastal plain, all the way to Florida.
This gently rolling plain begins across the Christina,
less than a half mile away, a region suited to large
plantations and the profitable use (in earlier days)
of slavery. Here economic and social life could be,
and often was, organized on a southern basis and on a
feudal principle. A shallop leaving the Brandywine
mills, an industrialized region with a hinterland of
owner-worked farms, could moor in the Christina,
a few miles away, or in creeks of the Delaware below,
to the landing wharf of a southern plantation. There
are roads from the Brandywine to the Christina
through what was Quaker, abolitionist country, that,
just across a bridge, run into flatlands where slaves
worked and their cabins still remain. I know nowhere
in the United States where there was, and is, so sudden a change in geography as at the mouth of the
Brandywine. Even in my youth, "downstate," which
meant everything below the Christina including New
Castle and the capital, Dover, was felt to be a different world, socially and intellectually, from industrial
Wilmington with its strong Quaker strain.

Thus the river's geography ends in the great Wilmington marshes, and the coastal plain. Five miles below is New Castle, old and lovely town, seventeenth and early eighteenth century capital of the whole region. It has been dying pleasantly for two hundred years, and now is being happily preserved as a museum of the colonial. At New Castle, the Delaware river begins to be a bay, and ninety miles farther south are the capes and the open ocean.

Up this bay with its marshy shores in 1638 came the *Kolmar Nyckel* and the yacht, *Vogel Grip,* with their cargo of pioneer Swedes and Finns, who, looking for firm ground on which to land, sailed on the Christina past the entrance to the Brandywine, and found, at last, a low rocky bluff on the very channel itself, with a prong of high land behind it. This bluff was the now famous Rocks, much cut down from their former eminence.

There they landed, built their fort and tiny town, and may have been the first white men, in their exploring, to see the Brandywine. But this is improbable, for the Dutchman De Vries had, earlier, attempted a settlement on the Delaware. And wandering Dutch or English, looking for furs, or prisoners of the Indians, must have crossed its stream below or above the Great Falls near tidewater. In any case, the Brandywine first appears in printed history as the Fishkill of the Swedes and the Dutch, running into Minquas Creek, named for trading Indians, and later rechristened Christina. Since the history of this settlement of New Sweden has been described in at least four good books, I shall not repeat it here, except when it touches the Brandywine. It is Delaware rather than Brandywine history.

The Fishkill is said to have had two Indian names, the Wawaset (spelled also Wawassan, Wawasiungh) for the lower river and the Suspecough for the upper stream above the gorge. There is an obvious error in this record of tradition. Suspecough, in the language of the river Indians, means a marshy creek. It could have been applied only to the estuary of the Brandywine, and would have best fitted the Christina. Since the Brandywine, for the Indians, as later quarrels show, was pre-eminently a spawning river up whose rapids vast shoals of edible fish ran every spring and fed the tribe, it is a fair guess that Wawaset was their name for the stream, at least above tidewater.

The Brandywine takes all the spill of the Welsh Hills east of the Susquehanna watershed and west of the drop to the Schuylkill, and gathers contributory streams from much of the Chester County country of hills and valleys. Thus it has always been subject to turbulent floods. I have seen the little river raging

through its Wilmington canyon, its dams mere ripples in a yellow, roaring torrent. Bridges, races, and
mills have suffered time and again, but the valley is
too narrow, the exit in broad marshes too relieving,
to endanger much property or life. Nevertheless, this
habitual flooding has produced, above the gorge or
canyon, meadowlands, lush, flowery, rich for grazing, and has been responsible, since the earliest days
when the Swedes with their red cattle began to work
inland, for a dairy industry which accounts for the
evidences of long-time prosperity—solid houses of
stone, great stone barns, and trim acres—in all this
Brandywine country. Indeed, once the observer is
north of the forested canyon of the New Castle
County hills, what he will inevitably remember best
of the Brandywine are these deep meadows, long
rather than broad, studded often with vast trees large
enough to stand up against the rush of floodwaters,
their soil renewed semiannually by rising water, and
given over, except for an occasional and precarious
crop of corn, to fat cattle that stray lazily through
the deep grass or lie in the shade of the isolated trees.
And, next to the meadows, and caused by the same
phenomenon of geography, he will remember the
water-loving sycamores, characteristic tree of the
Brandywine, that line the banks, bend over the water,
or, toppled by the floods, lie in the river itself, like

amphibians with roots still in land and branches fluttering over the current.

The early historical evidences of men's interest in the Brandywine are obscure, and usually indirect. As roads, railroads, and ranges of hills cross it always, so did travelers, who seldom followed its course. Fish, dams, fords, bridges, and the rights of an Indian tribe are the first concerns. Few rivers of equal length can have more bridges. And no such river has more millsites. A pastoral stream through much of its length, a wild stream still in many stretches, the use of power, and its peculiar geography, made it part of our economic history.

CHAPTER THREE

Primitive River

OUR immigrant ancestors of the first generation had no eye for scenery. They were seeking furs and gold and other exportable products or cultivatable and defensible land. And even of land the Dutch traders, who explored the Delaware region first, seem to have been ignorant, like the townsmen and adventurers who first settled New England and Virginia. They came to trade, not to live by agriculture. The Swedish and Finnish peasants, who arrived at the mouth of Brandywine in 1638, knew how to handle and subdue a wilderness. Of all the early settlers, they were the best for clearing and improving the soil, but they were illiterate except for their leaders, and have left no records of their environment except the indirect references in the memoirs of their educated ministers.

There are a number of early descriptions of Delaware Bay and the great river, but most of them quite unspecific. We hear of Paradise Point near Cape Henlopen, so called for its leafy beauty by the sea-weary voyagers on the *Key of Colmar* and the *Vogel Grip* who landed for refreshment there in the spring of 1638. The land in that region of pines, sand, oaks, and rich shrubbery must then have been in bloom.

The most specific account of the Brandywine estuary in earliest times is to be found in the memoir of Peter Mŏrtensson Lindeström, the Swedish engineer who wrote the story of the siege of Christinaham (the fort and settlement on the Rocks of Christina) by Peter Stuyvesant's invading armada. But his map reaches only to the Great Falls at tidewater of the Brandywine. If any Swede had gone farther, he had brought no news back as to the course of the stream.

This is not surprising. The Swedes settled first by the marshes and open meadowlands near the Delaware, which was their highway and protection. Only very slowly did they push into the interior, and then the Brandywine, a wild river in an unmanageable, uncultivatable gorge, would not have been their easiest route. It was good only for fish, of which there were plenty everywhere. And above its canyon was Indian country. They went west along the dead water of the Christina, north, south, and across on the Delaware, but left alone, so far as any evidence goes, the Brandywine, with its woods and upper Indian cornfields, for at least a generation.

We are fortunate, however, in a source which, while much later than the settlement of New Sweden, is, nevertheless, early enough for a traveler to have seen the Brandywine backwoods and equivalent regions in their primitive state, and this description is provided by a naturalist and geographer, not by an engineer or a captain of an expedition. Indeed, it is more expert and more detailed than any other descriptions of the American land written before the latter eighteenth century.

Peter Kalm, a Swede of Finnish descent, who would have called himself a botanist and agriculturist, was sent in 1748 by the Swedish Academy of Science to learn what he could, in what had once been New Sweden, of new plants and trees suitable for propagation in Sweden. His travels backward and forward through lower Pennsylvania, western New Jersey, and upper Delaware, with his longer journeys to the north, are recorded in a book translated into English in 1770, and recently revised and edited, with new material, by Adolph B. Benson. It is a gossipy record, rich in minute observation, and particularly valuable for us because Kalm took pains to search out the old Swedes still surviving from the original colony and to question them in their own tongue as to what the country was like in their youth and in the time of the first pioneers. Kalm also, in addition to being a scientific observer, was a conservationist. He deplored the erosion and exhaustion of good soil from hasty farming, already visible in the older regions, the destruction of forests near the settlements, the depletion of many natural resources, and made constant comparisons with the state of New Sweden before the havoc began. While he seems to have known the Brandywine only at its mouth, and at the ford which crossed above the first falls, his careful description of near-by territory makes it possible to reconstruct for the imagination the Brandywine of the seventeenth century—a primitive American river.

The handiest way to such a description is by narrative, and fictitious narrative, though it would prove to be fictitious only in an assembling of probable incident. I will choose the spring of 1643. Five years before, the Swedes had built the stockaded port of Christinaham on the Rocks of the Christina Creek. In February of 1643, Governor Printz, newly sent from the home country, had sailed his four hundred pounds of valorous flesh up the river to take command of the colony. Two years before his arrival, restless New Haveners from Connecticut, disappointed in profits from their trade and perhaps in the climate of their southern New England, had settled some twenty families on the east side of the great river, where Salem Creek enters the estuary. Printz, in 1643, was building a fort there to be sure that English expansion in his New Sweden went no farther, but he had been ordered to use no force, and the New Haveners had reason to hope that, between Dutch claims and Swedish possession, they might yet succeed in forming a colony of a colony. Indeed, a few years later it was proposed in New Haven town meeting that the river settlement, if successful, should have equal rights in government with New Haven, becoming a second capital in which (as with New Haven and Hartford later) the assembly should meet in alternate years. This was not to be. In 1643, in spite of deeds they held from the Indians, these pioneers were precariously settled under the protection of the Swedish commander, whose purpose it was to ease them out gently and get them to go home "as more expedient for the interest of her majesty, Queen Christina." Finally he got them out, and himself too, for his Fort Elfsborg near their settlement was literally captured by clouds of mosquitoes. The New Haveners, hardened by the fierce tribe of the Quinnipiac marshes, seem to have had tougher hides than the Swedes.

Alien to the Dutch and Swedes in what was to become an English-speaking country, these Englishmen had a short-term interest in immediate profits and a long-term hope for permanent settlement. Already New Haveners had tried to open up the profitable fur trade with the Susquehanna Indians from a blockhouse on the Schuylkill, and had been driven away, with heavy losses in goods, by the Dutch from New Amsterdam under Governor Kieft. The same hope must have been alive in the Salem colony. For there were no furs of value in the warm and sandy New Jersey hinterland, nor indeed much fur of quality in all the mild river region. Good fur came from the mountains to the north and the west, a wilderness where the Iroquois ruled.

The place, then, is Salem Creek in late May of 1643. A dugout of some twenty feet in length, hollowed by burning from a white-cedar log, is being pushed from its hiding place in a mass of honeysuckle. Two Indians of the river tribes are swinging it toward an open bank. They are Algonquins by speech and blood, called Mantas by the Swedes, although closely akin to, if not actually a part of, the Lenni-Lenape nation that inhabits the upper river. All these river Indians were loosely federated, and even the dark Nanticokes of the southern peninsula came later to be called Delawares when the slow aggression of the whites pushed the remnants of all the tribes into the faraway northwest.

But these Indians are still proud and independent savages. They wear loincloths of buckskin, leggings and moccasins, and wampum bands holding quivers of arrows are slung across their shoulders. Their faces are lightly painted for they are off to the meeting place of other races in Minquas Creek. The Swedes are their friends, and they themselves belong to a

friendly race, generous and childlike, though easily
made suspicious, and then violent and unexpected in
action. The English have offered them knives and
little bells to be their guides, but they are not at ease
with them as with the Swedes. And, indeed, the two
New Haven traders keep their guns in their hands
until the spears and bows of the Indians are in the
canoe, and one watches on guard until the other has
taken his place. Could even a peaceful Indian be
trusted? I do not know their names, but think they
may have been Nathaniel Turner and George Lamberton, who had sailed a sloop down from New Haven in 1641 and bought the Salem land from the
sachems. They would be town bred, like most of the
New Haveners, still unaccustomed to the wilderness, though dressed, like their new neighbors the
Swedes, in deerskin trousers and waistcoats, with caps
also of skin.

The broad misty bay into which the Indians
shoot the clumsy dugout with unexpected speed is
bright with May sunlight and rippling from a faint
ocean breeze. Herons flap and cranes stalk along the
muddy beaches they are leaving behind them, and
the marshes are musical with song and noisy with
whistles and quackings of waterfowl. Millions of
ducks have already gone northward with geese and
swans, but there seem to be millions more bedding on

the water or flying in straight lines among the curving gulls and terns. The bay breaks with the roll and
splash of great sturgeon running toward fresh water
and leaping as they go, 300-pounders some of them.

It is a long paddle across the blue bay to the
reedy shoals of the western shore of the river, which
stretches north and south as far as they can see in a
line of forest broken only by a few sandy beaches and
a single thread of smoke from what seems to be a
meadow and a clearing. The view is empty of human
life, except for a single canoe moving slowly through
a marshy channel of the shore, a dark-skinned native
at the bow with upraised spear. "Nanticoke," the
Indian paddlers grunt, and swing their dugout from
shore, yet hail as they go past. The white men lift
their guns, but drop them quickly. They have already
learned that on the Delaware the practice of regard-
ing the Indian as a devil best exterminated does not
prevail. The Swedes have lived in peace and fair exchange with them and, like the French, have become
half Indian themselves. There are no Indian wars on
the Delaware. If the land has been sold and resold
again and again to Dutch, Swedes, and English, that
is because the sachems have no sense of private property and sell only its communal use—there is, after
all, so much of it!—and have already got smallpox
and measles and too many neighbors as a price. Yet

the Swedes and Finns have been good neighbors bringing wonderful gifts, and are brave but not grasping. First the Indians fed them, but now depend on the white man's better cultivated fields for much of their winter corn.

Lamberton and Turner, looking ahead, see already the rising hills above the marshy bay of Minquas Creek, now renamed the Christina. They hope for a chance to trade with the Susquehannas, who should be bringing in their northern skins, and staying to collect wild peas (golden club) from the river marshes, while the Swedes preserve the peace of the trading place. For the river Indians fear these tall and fierce Iroquois and would ambush them if they dared.

The river has narrowed to three miles across, the hills to the westward have lifted, and now in a semicircle they bound a long marshy bay, with a narrow, but deep, entrance from the river. On the firm ground to the north are a few log cabins at the forest edge, where some Swedes have enlarged Indian fields. Canoes are moving in the winding channels of the creeks. With a grunt and a heave the Indian paddlers swing the heavy dugout inland and enter the Christina. Already they can see, across the reed-flecked waves of the marsh, a point of land carrying a square stockade, buttressed at its corners, with the roofs of cabins visible within. Cleared land, with some log cabins, the beginnings of the little town of Christinaham, rises behind to the heavy trees of the untouched forest. And beyond and above only forest and the hills.

Paddling fast now, the Mantas push the dugout, with a wave at its prow, toward a muddy beach under the Rocks and the stockade where a dozen similar craft and one ship's boat are already pulled out from the water or are tied by grapevine ropes to the bushes beneath the terrace. As their bow slides up on the muddy reeds there is a stir of interest on the slopes above, and a chorus of grunts as the two Englishmen climb out with their guns.

On the terrace before the stockade, groups of river Indians are squatting around cooking fires. A Swedish sentry in a cloth coat paces between them and the half-opened gate of the stockade. At the end of his beat is a rough log cabin, near the water's edge, which is steaming at every crack as if a deer were being boiled whole therein. Its door bursts open, and four naked Swedes, shouting with mirth and beating their bare, red bodies with branches, run across the terrace and dive into the river. A woman follows, equally nude, but seeing white strangers, hurries back into the bathhouse.

The Mantas are already talking to the other river Indians, but as the New Haveners hesitate, not know-

ing whether to try their English on the sentry or trust
the Indians to get what information they need, there
is a whoop from up the Christina, and a rush from
the fires for bows and arrows. The sentry fires his
gun. Soldiers—barefoot and ragged—come piling
from inside the stockade, and a cry goes up, echoed
from cabin to cabin behind the walls, "Minquas!
Minquas!"

The traders, running with the rest to the southern edge of the Rocks, see a line of dugouts paddling
down the Christina. Already the leading canoe is near
enough for them to note that the paddlers are large
men, differently painted from the Lenape, white pre-
vailing in their faces. When they land, one sees that
they are taller and longer of face than the river Indians, over six feet some of them, and of superior
bearing. They lift hands of peace to the soldiers, but
look over the Lenapes' heads as if they were not there.
And, indeed, the Lenapes, and the New Haveners'
Mantas with them, withdraw a little, leaving an open
space before the gates, on which now are dumped
bundles from the arriving canoes, which are carried
up the banks by squaws dressed in buckskin skirts
below their naked breasts, while the men keep watch
with bows and spears. The New Haveners nod to
each other, "The Susquehannas," and step nearer to

watch the packs of skins unroll—beaver, otter, lynx, deer, mink, bear, and bunches of dried tobacco.

Crossing the gap in the westerly hills, following the trail to tidewater on the Christina, the Susquehannas have brought their winter's catch and spring trade with tribes of north and west to the whites for bargaining. Blood relations, though enemies, of the Mohawks, Oneidas, and Senecas, they are a powerful, warlike race, controlling not only the Susquehanna valley and the mountains above it, but also the trade routes to the far countries from which the Eries and the Neutrals, Iroquois like themselves, pass on valuable furs. The Swedes are their friends also, have, indeed, risked death and starvation in the unknown hinterland to secure their trade for themselves, in rivalry with the Dutch. It is a triumph for Governor Printz to have diverted so large a party from the trading path leading to New Amsterdam. The river Indians keep close to their Swedish protectors. All use sign language. For here Algonquin, Iroquois, and Europeans meet.

The factor of the Swedish company brings out his wares—bells, blankets, mirrors, and long Swedish knives, which are seen with grunts of desire by the Indians, some powder and lead, a tiny keg of brandewijn. This is a rich show of goods, for Printz has come well provided. Control hereabouts still depends

upon trade, for land titles mean nothing to the savages, who still could shove the settlers into the ocean
if they could overcome their own greed for brass pots,
bright knives, and cloth to keep them warm, and
whichever group of settlers can offer the most and
best has best assurance of safety as well as of profits.
Holland is still a great sea power. Sweden is still the
first military state in Europe. New England, Virginia,
and Maryland are still no more than clearings on the
edge of a great forest owned by no dominant power.

But now the great Printz himself, a figure made
for the brush of Franz Hals and the pen of Rabelais,
trundles his weight to the Indian circle, but stops at
the sight of strange white faces. He knows the English, that restless wave already lapping downward
from New England and upward from Maryland,
and can command a dog Latin not too difficult for a
New Havener to understand. The Minquas trade belongs to the Swedes. Let the New Haveners go back
to their shore of the river, and, better still, to New
England.

It is twilight. Lamberton and Turner, with a
wistful look at the ground strewn with furs, and a
jealous sniff at the odors of cooking and of brandewijn borne out of the stockade on the smoke of many
fires, push off reluctantly into the Christina. But if
the front door to the Minquas country is bolted

against them, there may be a back way. That wild south-running stream, the Fishkill, of which they had heard, what if one followed to its upper waters and over the divide to the Susquehanna! It was said to flow into the marsh; indeed, they had passed a river mouth before they reached the Rocks. Rounding a curve which took them out of sight of the port, they see a broad channel leading toward the hills, and, this time, gesture the Indians into it. Paddling in the dusk, they soon hear the roar of rapids ahead, while on their right the marsh rises into firm land heavily timbered. Landing amidst frightened beach birds and whirring partridges, they find dry woods remote from the busy fort into which the Swedes shut themselves at night. Here, on Timber Island on the Brandywine, which was to become the residence site of the next Swedish governor, they spend the night.

In a misty dawn they are on their way toward the roar of the Great Falls. Between banks suddenly become steep they paddle through the last pool of the estuary to the end of a rapids coming from as far above as they could see. The Indians murmur "Wawassan." They were not falls at all, so they see, but a slide of waves tumbling among rocks, too steep and too rough to paddle up or even, so they think, to pole the canoe. The Indians think so too, it is clear, and must have known this beginning of the real river, for

they steer to shore, pull the heavy dugout into a
tunnel of spicewood where a tiny stream enters,
and take out their weapons and the heavy traders'
packs.

There was a faint trail behind the maples, gums,
and sycamores that hung over the western edge of
the dashing river until their branches were flicked by
the waves. It is there still, and I have often followed
it over carpets of dogtooth violet in early spring, and
through Johnny-jump-ups and wild geraniums in
May and June. It climbs uphill over rocks and dives
into thickets of ironwood and wild cherry, and sometimes takes to steppingstones in the river itself at the
foot of some ledge of granite. Up this, a Mantas leading with bow in hand, the traders with their guns
and packs, a Mantas in the rear with a roll of blankets
and another of food slung by a tump line from his
forehead, they climb, twist, and struggle.

Their eyes are on the trail, yet even the traders
are aware of the beauty of the place. Above the steep
slopes of the river canyon, the forest floor is still black
underfoot from the March fires of the Indians. They
had burned the underbrush so that the silently stepping game could be seen and driven toward hidden
hunters. The sight ran clear there to far away, under
magnificent columns of chestnut, oak, beech, linden,
and hickory, so widely spaced that an oxcart could be

driven anywhere over the forest floor, except where
ledges and fallen trunks were piled. But the fires had
not crossed the ravines made by descending streams
and, there, the vast trunks of tulip trees rose to crown
all above the forest. Nor had the flames descended
the moist slopes and margins of the river, which were
covered with an impenetrable tangle of briars, honeysuckle, spicewood, wild cherries, and wild plums in
sweet bloom, while, looped and flung over all, and
climbing the high trees and spraying out over the
river itself, the wild grape raced. So violent was the
competition for light that the trees at the water's
edge burst into crowns of foliage far out over the
rapids. On the steep opposing slope the dogwood was
flowering brilliantly, and a single tulip tree, on a
clifftop, rose so high that from its top one could
surely see the fort at the Rocks, and the distant Jersey
shore, and the shimmer of the bay to the south, beyond which lay the ocean.

The bulky packs, forced through the river thickets, dislodge innumerable birds: Maryland yellow-
throats, Carolina wrens, yellow warblers, to whom
this lower region belongs. Orioles are building in the
pendent branches, and hummingbirds dart from the
pink azalea blossoms in the shrubbery to their tiny
lichened nests on the limbs of the trees that overhang
the water. Cardinals, water thrushes, wood thrushes,

ovenbirds are all musical, for it is still the early morning hour of song. The explorers see a brilliant wood duck floating in a backwater, and an osprey winging up the ripples, with an eagle soaring above him ready to seize his prey.

It is high water but not flood. At the head of the rapids the gorge widens into sunlight and the trail takes to a water meadow beside a slow-moving pool, and here the traders halt to shift their packs. "A mill-site," says Lamberton, and here, indeed, the famous chain of Brandywine mills was to begin. Here, also, a branch trail turns down to the water, which shallows into a flood. Thirty years later, George Fox, with all of Quakerism in his heart, was to ride his stumbling horse across this ford, but only Indians have used it so far. The Swedes keep to the great river. Upstream is the traders' way to the Minquas country, and they sign to lift packs and turn north toward the sound of falling water.

But the Indians grunt and point toward the pool and then lead the white men to a ledge above the slow current. The water is clear but faintly golden, like brandewijn, or Dutch gin,[1] cask drawn, from which, by a pleasant legend of a liquor-laden ship sunk by ice in the estuary, the river was supposed to have got

---

[1] The liquor referred to by the Swedes as brandewijn seems to have been a gin, although the word (which is Dutch) is now used in Holland for brandy.

its name. It is legend only, for one Brantwyn, a Swede, was soon to take up land on the lower river, which was to be called his creek—a less romantic but more probable source for the mellifluous name. Yet, distilled from a hundred valleys, the water runs brandy clear today, and through its currents are darting thousands of little fishes, packing the channels of the rapids below and spreading in gleaming shadows through the pool—alewives running up to their spawning grounds. Good to eat, better to grow corn with, the Indians explain with hands and mouth.

A splash in the upper waters of the pool draws all eyes, and now they see that the smooth surface is momentarily broken by hundreds of curving lines, formed with the speed of the wind. The Indians mumble a name, and greedily rub their stomachs. Now the white men can see thousands of dim shapes, faintly silvered with luminous patches, and some of great length, that restlessly move in bands through the current or, as if by signal, shoot across, up, down the pool, troubling its waters with their periscopic fins. The buck shad have come up from the ocean and are fighting for places on the spawning bed. There are spotted trout in the river too, and one leaping salmon who has lost his way, for it is too far south for the icy lakes in which his kind breeds; and one sturgeon also who rolls and splashes like a sport-

ive submarine, and shows his ugly snout. Fishkill the
river is called, and rightly.

Now they are entering a steeper canyon where
the river narrows, curves, and roars down its rapids.
A cliff of weathered granite overhangs the entrance,
its crevices awave with wildflowers. The thicket is of
laurel now, with tenacious arms, the spoonwood of
the Indians, and indeed the leading Indian cuts a
branch with his Swedish knife and whittles its ivory-
textured wood as he goes.

The Brandywine, now below them, is lashing
round great upright rocks. The forest is heavy and
dark, the path rough and hard on moccasined feet.
It is a relief to come out in the sunlight on a little
beach at the foot of a long slide of rippling water.
But the Indians crouch and pull the traders back into
the bushes. Halfway up the slide, which was to become Hagley dam, a black bear squats on a rock with
one paw poised above the eddy over a pothole. He
strikes sharply at the water, and scoops out a two-
foot wriggling shad, throws it over his shoulder into
the bushes, and wades back into the forest before the
guns are ready.

At the top of the falls is a long, deep pool syca-
more-shaded on its margins. On its grassy bank they
sit down to rest, and eat of the dried meat and
parched maize they have brought with them. Across,

a solid wall of foliage lifts from the water's edge. It parts like a curtain, and a great head, with spreading velvety horns, and soft eyes looking at the cool water, emerges for a moment, snuffs at the faint air, and as slowly withdraws. It is the elk, the great stag of which they have heard, but never seen in New England or to the east of the great river. Farther up the pool a doe, of the smaller deer kind, steps daintily into the shallows, sniffs the same tainted air, and with a flip of her white tail, bounds up into the willows.

The Mantas talk together, point ahead, and then increase the pace as if headed for some known destination before evening. Scrambling over still rougher rocks, the party, after an hour's going, reaches the foot of a heavy fall that marks the end of the canyon. Beyond is sunlight and a grassy meadow and easy going under spread willows for a mile or two until, with cautious steps, the lead Indian steps down into the shallows and points to the mouth of an entering stream on the other side. Beside it is a rough field, the first sign of human life they have seen since leaving Christinaham. The Indians whoop but there is no reply. Searching through the masses of honeysuckle and ivy on the bank, they find and pull out a small dugout, load the packs on it, and wade the stream arm-pit high, pushing the canoe before them. The field is small and stinks of rotting alewives piled on the hills of corn. Shoots of corn and rows of tiny plants are pushing through the roughly turned soil. Two digging sticks lie dropped between the rows. The Mantas name the rows to each other, with expressive gestures, easily understood. There is the maize, and squash vines between the hills, and beans, and tobacco, and sunflowers along the edges.

A trail leads up the brook which the white men, leaving their packs, follow after the Indians, who have set arrows to their bows. It is a dark and narrow valley under immense tulip trees and pin oaks, with a floor as open as a park. Uphill they can see sunlight, and the white of falling water, and soon a rough dam of cut sticks across the stream, which the Indians approach with noiseless steps. When they have crawled through the brush and come to the water's edge, all that is to be seen is a marshy pond, with one gaunt heron stalking in the shallows. But along the edge are the conical tops of what Lamberton and Turner guess to be beaver houses, made of cut sticks and branches, and while they watch in silence, a brown head, with a black snout and dark amber eyes, rises, cuts a quick V across the pond, and with an enormous splash from a flat tail, disappears. "How catch him?" Turner asks in pantomime. An Indian sweeps the sun down with a gesture, strains his eyes as peering through the dusk, and draws his bow. Then he jumps up, and wading into the water below one of the houses, feels about subaqueously until he finds a length of rope made from the wild hemp, and pulls up a crude iron trap. Dutch from its look, say the New Englanders. It is baited with a shrubby branch of heavy glaucous leaves, which they recognize as the sweet bay, or little magnolia, seen flowering in the Salem swamps. The Indian's gestures make clear that this is the candy and caviar of the beaver. Trappers and beaver between them seem to have used up this southern shrub, for I have never encountered it in my ramblings on the Brandywine, in whose neighborhood Kalm and others saw it in some abundance.

Back at the cornfield, they shoulder packs and trot north along the east bank of the Brandywine, looking, so the whites guess, for the owners of the cornfield. Grunting expressively, the Mantas point to moccasin prints on the damp soil of the woods. The trail climbs up a wooded bluff, and comes out into the light on a broad ledge overlooking a thousand yards of rippling river. Now they see why the field was deserted. Below them, the Brandywine has spread into rippling shallows, two hundred feet from bank to bank. Across the shoals a deep V of rocks has been built, just high enough to break the hurrying water. It points downstream and is open for a channel, a few feet broad, at the bottom. Knee-deep on either side of the opening stand two bronze and naked Indians, eyes on the current, each with a forked spear poised. Along the arms of the V on the downstream side, a dozen men and women in loincloths only, are splashing with long saplings tied at the end to make crude nets. "Achquaveman," say the Mantas. With these fish brooms they sweep the shallows. Above the V, children are paddling about with drawn bows, or little spears, prodding the holes between the rocks, or diving, arms spread, into the river. While the New Haveners are watching silently, screams and shouts rise from the fishers. The bronze watchers at the dam gate dart their spears, and each lifts a flapping shad, which is shaken off into a hempen net held up by the nearest squaw. A rush of shad is coming up the river. Now the fish brooms begin to toss gleaming, twisting fish over the heads of the fishers to the shore, and soon a child above falls on a shad, lifts it hugged tight to his naked belly, and is rolled fish and all over into the current while all shout with laughter. Shad are flapping among the grass and ferns of the bank, and children are tossing them into baskets held by tump lines on the backs of squaws.[1]

"Ho!" calls the lead Indian, loud enough to carry over the noise of running water. Laughter and move-

[1] For various details in this account, I am indebted to newspaper communications from Amos C. Brinton, preserved in the Delaware Historical Society archives.

ment cease on the river, except for the two spearsmen
at the chute who leap to shore to pick up their bows.
"Ho," they cry distrustfully, but are reassured by
words of greeting from the rock above. Soon men,
women, and children, carrying baskets full of thrash-
ing shad, or hauling silvery fish after them by grapevine cords tied to the gills, climb up to the trail, stare
at the white men, talk to the guides with friendly
voices, and beckon along the path. They are un-
painted, and, except for bows, unarmed. A naked
child touches Lamberton's gun barrel curiously, then
bawls at the unfamiliar whiteness of the face above
him. All laugh. They seem a good-natured lot.

A mile or so above, the Brandywine swings in a
noble curve beneath a steep and stony hill, later
called Point Lookout, on the boundary line between
Delaware and Pennsylvania. Embraced by the curve
is a water meadow, dry, and deep in grass and flowers,
and in it is pitched the summer fishing camp of perhaps a hundred Lenape. Their winter town is above
the Forks of the river and inland. A village has been
set up under the meadow trees and close to the river.
The wigwams are only poles supporting strips of
bark, with deerskins hung from the eaves to keep out
the rain. In the middle of each hut, a fire is burning
and there are piles of furs and mats woven of rushes
for sleeping. With shouts of racing children and bark-

ing of dogs, the traders are led into the midst of the
camp, and given a hut and mats for the night now
approaching—four noble shad also to add to their
corn and dried venison. An old sachem, with a Dutch
medal hung on his wampum band, comes to give
them ceremonious greetings, and the traders respond
with gifts. He leaves for them woolly robes of some
strange skin, which, after argument, they decide come
from the wild cattle or buffalo of the mountains to
the west and south; said to be heavy beasts and un-
tamable, their pelts of little value except for warmth.

The Mantas parboil their shad on the coals, and
gulp down everything but backbone and head, spit-
ting bones as they eat. The white men, finding a roe
in one of their fish, give it to the dogs as probably
poisonous, and eat more carefully. The May night
grows dark and cool, with the cry of the night bird,
the whippoorwill, in chorus all about the camp, and
howlings of wolves on the opposite hill, answered by
the dogs. The sachem comes to sit by their fire, lights
with a coal a stone pipe with a reed stem three feet
long, passes it to Lamberton and Turner, puffs it
again himself, then courteously withdraws. Their own
Indians join a tribal circle, smoke, sing, chatter half
through the night, while the traders, feeling reason-
ably safe, sleep well.

At dawn, with a drink of spring water, and a

handful of maize to chew, they take the river trail again, and are well away from the camp before the sun breaks through the mists. The river banks are fluttering with wings, plovers and swallows whirl up and down the current, kingfishers splash and rattle, a scarlet tanager drops like a burning coal from a high oak into the bushes. Fawns trip to the edge and drink, and on the steep hillside across the river, well out of range, a splendid turkey cock struts in the sun, his wattles shining like ruby. And always in the amber water, they see the strong shad, breasting upward in troops or skittering madly across the pools.

Later, having pushed through a dense jungle of briers under spread sycamores, they come into the sunlight of wide meadows, parked with enormous trees, each set in a pool of shadow. It is good land, even though subject to floods. The white men look at it enviously. The pace is swift. Before noon they come to a fork in the river, and choosing the left way, as leading toward the Susquehanna country, they splash through below the rapids and soon find themselves headed west. But they have gone on less than a mile when both Indians take the lead, making a sign of trotting feet. Moving cautiously, they come, indeed, to a cross path, a beaten trail, very different from their obscure trace, broad and much used, and leading east and west. Suddenly their guides pull them back into hiding, covering their mouths with cupped hands. Noiseless, yet with precision, a file of Indians trot down the side trail. They are heavily painted and armed, their heads shaved to the scalp lock; yet each, by a tump line, carries a bundle of furs. By their height and the white paint on their faces, the New Haveners guess that they, also, are Susquehannas, out of their own territory, on the trading path leading to the Falls of the Delaware and New Amsterdam. Here was a through route to the Susquehanna country, but by a way too familiar to Swedes and Dutch. If there was to be a private entrance for forbidden Englishmen, it would be northward.

And so on through the afternoon they push through heightening hills, climb a winding pass, where the stream foams beside them, and soon, across a broad lateral valley, have glimpses of a misty range crossing from west to east. Sleeping under a hemlock by the bank, they are off by sunrise, and by noon have left the soft fertility of the low country behind them. The stream is now a mountain brook, which dashes down a stony slope, rough, rugged, grown in scrubby oak and chestnut, with rock gashes showing stains of red iron. The traders are puzzled. This is Connecticut country. They might be on their own hills back of West Rock. The trail has disappeared. The Indians are hesitant. But the obstinate traders push on west of north, still hoping for an entrance to the Minquas country. Minks steal up the bank ahead of them, wild pigeons flutter in the crooked trees. They climb higher, come to a place of divided rills, follow one to a spring, and then see above them light sky shining through the tree trunks and silvering the laurel undercover. It is the top of the range. And indeed, leaving the last water, and climbing a ridge of rock and yellow pine, they step out on a gap in the range, swept by a westerly breeze. There, with a "Ho!" the Indians stop and gesture westward. The land falls away at their feet in rolling forest, down and down to the glint of a broad river, backed by dim blue shapes of distant mountains. "Susquehanna," say the Mantas.

Just below them, a spring trickles out of a crevice and makes a little stream which flows into a ravine that becomes a valley leading toward the west. This was the back door to the Susquehannas, a possible route for traders who must smuggle past the Swedes at Christinaham! Up this pass with loads of fur, down to where the Brandywine became a river, then, on rafts in high water or by some short cut by land to the Delaware—that was the new trade route they believed they had found.

But the door is closed. The guides give no warning, nor seem surprised, when a dozen Indians, painted in the river colors, shaven like the Minquas, and with arms in hand, rise silently from the laurel scrub below them. They surround the traders with firm, if friendly, gestures. Their leader seems to be a man of authority, for the long pipe he waves toward them has a bowl carved into the similitude of a turkey, and the woven pouch slung across his chest glitters with a plaque of beaten copper. The words are few. If the white men from the east wish to trade, so they make out from the pantomime, let it be with their friends, the Lenape, who need knives and guns more than the Minquas, their enemies. Let the white men go back across the great river and furs will be brought to them. He is a chief of the Lenape: he names his name.

The white men turn back. But they had seen —surely they were the first Europeans to see—the course of the Brandywine! Nor do they go empty-handed. For the Indians call to them to return. From behind a rock the sachem lifts rolls of skins that, unbound, glisten with the watery shine of mountain otter and the soft glow of beaver. The packs of the New Haveners are untied. Trading begins.

CHAPTER FOUR

Indian Finale

FOR nearly half a century after 1643, the history of the Brandywine, except for one dramatic scene at its mouth, is Indian. Christinaham was a meeting and trading place for three Indian nations, the Lenni-Lenape, their relatives, the Nanticokes of the Peninsula, and their enemies, the Iroquoian Susquehannas, or Minquas. There seems to have been a fourth nation represented in trading and warfare, the "black Minquas," but no one knows who they were, though it is guessed that the Eries, also Iroquois, may have sent small trading parties over the Susquehanna routes and were called Minquas because they were Iroquois, and black from their ceremonial paint. But the Brandywine, from mouth to source, was in the territory of that tribe of the river Indians called Lenni-Lenape, which seems to mean the true, or the old, men. The Delawares, as all the river tribes came to be called, including the Lenape, were less warlike, less gregarious, and slightly less advanced in culture than the Iroquois, having passed not quite so far into an agricultural stage. From the beginning, the Delawares were known as the white man's friends. Chingachgook, the Delaware, was Deerslayer's companion; and, later, their scouts guided armies of the

59

United States across the plains, and Washington Irving on his western expedition.

The Brandywine seems to have been particularly
valued by the Lenape, as the history of the peculiar
land grants shows. It was their food river, their fish
supply, never failing until the white man interfered.
When the Swedes came, they seem to have been a
contented people, troubled only by raids of the Susquehannas from the west. But, though the Swedes
were good neighbors, the natives were rapidly re-
duced by the new European diseases, by strong drink
which they could not resist, and by the shrinkage of
their hunting grounds. Smallpox devastated the Minquas, and probably the river Indians also, in 1661 and
1662. About 1674, the Senecas, Iroquois from the
north, ended a period of warfare by utterly destroy-
ing the Susquehanna nation. After that the Lenni-
Lenape were left in peace, but the attrition of civilization was as disastrous as war.

Their cornfields on the Brandywine and the
shad that ran up in the spring were wealth to these
Indians, but they never fought for them. The Swedes
stuck to the shores of the great river, trading and
probably hunting with the Brandywine Indians, and
adopting many of their customs and some of their
weapons and garments. But they kept out of their
inland territory until the English, more aggressive

and more numerous, began to buy and open up the land.

The great purchase in 1683 by William Penn from the Indians included, directly or indirectly, the Brandywine valley from the settlement at its mouth to its sources. He bought from the Indians all lands in this region of which they still claimed ownership, with certain exceptions. The Indian town above the Forks of the Brandywine was certainly not intended to be included in this sale, for the Indians violently protested later that their rights there were being invaded. There seems also to have been a reservation for the river itself. In 1705, the Delaware chiefs insisted that they had been given a deed from Penn conveying to them a mile on each side of the Brandywine from its mouth up the west branch to its source in the Welsh Hills. This deed, they said, was unfortunately burnt by a fire in a hut. There is no final evidence of its existence, but the fact seems probable. It was fishing rights evidently that they wished to secure, along a river which in the 1680's was completely wild in that portion of its gorge which ran through Swedish Delaware, and entirely unsettled above. The commissioners of property of the province for 1706 evidently believed in the justice of the claim, or of some agreement, since by payment of £100 they extinguished the two-mile reservation up as far as a rock

on the west branch just above the Forks (now quar-
ried away, but marked) and confirmed the rest of the
grant. A parallel case to this dependence upon fishing
rights may be the final settlement of the Stockbridge
Indians on the barren west side of the Housatonic
below Kent in Connecticut, where, nevertheless, the
falls and pools of that part of the river would have
provided sustenance when the salmon and shad were
running.

But trouble for this Lenni-Lenape remnant soon
began. They were peaceful, in spite of rumors of war
among settlers greedy for land and ready to believe
the worst of their Indian neighbors as long as they
still owned anything. About 1688, Caleb Pusey, a
courageous Quaker, and pamphleteer for his people,
went alone to the Indian town on the Brandywine,
where, so the warmongers said, five hundred war-
riors were encamped and ready to descend upon Philadelphia. He found a lame king being cared for by his
wives, and children playing among the huts. It was
these children that the Lenni-Lenape later petitioned
should never be sold into slavery.

Soon the settlers, pushing westward from Philadelphia, began to buy and sell land even on the reservation of the west-branch waters, and to survey in
the Indian town. In great dignity, the Indians came
to the Assembly asking for protection. Not only were

their lands threatened, but by dams and weirs, especially in the lower waters of the river near its mouth, the shad and other migratory fish were being stopped in their run. Their children, said the Indians, who had captured the shad with their bows and arrows, were being wantonly starved. In 1725 and again in 1726 they were promised redress, but nothing was done. The governor said he would go to New Castle and prosecute the dam builders, but nothing was done. Indeed, in 1729, Checochinican, a chief, complained that his people were not even allowed to cut wood on their lands for the cabins of their town. We can see the aristocratic dignity of these sachems of the Delawares in the portraits of some of them by Gustavus Hesselius, a really distinguished Swedish painter, who began his American career in Maryland and Delaware in 1711.[1]

There was a mill on the Brandywine at the Great Falls in the seventeenth century, but it probably had no dam. The one that Samuel Kirks built at the Falls in 1727, taking over this earlier Swedish site, had a short race and an undershot wheel, and probably rocks and logs were piled across the top of the rapids in preparation, so as to divert enough water into the race. This would have discouraged the shad,

[1] See Johnson's edition of Lindeström.

who are not good leapers, and may have caused the Indians' complaint.

The Indians gave up in the 1750's. When the French and Indian Wars, so called, began, the Delawares were urged by the French to desert their English friends. The alliance with the English was re-established, and the river Indians were not in any case affected, but after frontier bloodshed and white treachery, and the spread of general distrust, the chiefs of what was left of the river tribes had enough. In 1757 a melancholy pilgrimage began, the Nanticokes, far south on the Peninsula, joining the Lenni-Lenape. Carrying the bones of their ancestors with them, the Delaware nation moved over the ranges to the valleys of the Wyoming and Wyalusing, in the wild north of Pennsylvania. A handful of Nanticokes stayed behind and have left descendants in southern Delaware; one or two families remained on the Brandywine, whose last descendant, Indian Hannah, died on the ancestral lands in 1803. Graves are still there, some of them, by faithful agreement, never opened, but if descendants of the fishing Indians of the Brandywine still survive, they will be found in Canada or Oklahoma.

The Indians could not save the Brandywine fish. Their successors in the valley were more aggressive, but, in the long run, equally unsuccessful. As early as

1738, Abraham Marshall had built a dam on the west branch that offended the Indians. But when the great power sites by Wilmington began to be developed, the upper river had passed into the hands of Quaker farmers, and these did not propose to be deprived of the fish that still must have run upstream in some quantity. In 1756, on petition, a committee of New Castle County, Delaware, and Chester County, Pennsylvania farmers were authorized to inspect the Brandywine dams, see that fishways were left open, and break through the dams if they were not. What happened upstream I do not know, but when they reached the dam which Major Eliot had built near what is now Augustine in Wilmington, they ran into trouble. The major was on his dam in full regimentals, waving his broadsword. The Quaker farmers would not fight; but neither would they run. It looked like a day of wet feet for the major, until he thought of an expedient. The committee was invited up the hill to his house to drink a punch made of hard cider and cherry bounce. As a result, the dam was laid on the shelf for that year. But in 1760 another commission breached four dams, the major's among them. We hear of no more dam wars, but also of no more shad. Power was now dominant on the lower river. In spite of the committees, the fish were somewhere turned back. But so strong is the migratory instinct that in my youth I have seen herring or alewives packing by thousands the rapids of what were the Great Falls, vainly trying to get past the bulwarks of dams and races that block the ancient fishways of the Fishkill.[1]

Hannah, the last of the Brandywine Indians, lived alone with her two dogs, living by the sale of baskets which she dyed herself—some green and purple from unknown native sources—and by Indian medicine. When she went her rounds, her dog and pig went with her, and the dog could be sent to heel by calling "Cotch-a-mingo"—the Mingos or Minquas, the ancient enemies of her race, being thus used to frighten into obedience the last of the Indian dogs. She had a "proud and lofty spirit," says Joseph L. Lewis, early historian of Chester County, and "spoke emphatically of the wrongs and misfortunes of her people."

[1] See note on page 49.

CHAPTER FIVE

The Log Cabin Comes to America

WHEN I was a boy on the Brandywine, I discovered, so I thought, the relics of an early and adventurous history. I was reading about adventures of the pioneers, and the log cabin, that symbol of frontier life, was, in my imagination, the center of every dramatic scene, arrows quivering in its chinks, bursts of flame and powder smoke from its narrow windows, a savage on the roof trying to find entrance, another with a tomahawk behind the nearest forest oak. Yet in that peaceful Quaker country, cultivated to its last rich acre, where even the forests were parklike, log cabins were still not rare. Sometimes they stood alone in a shabby acre, and were inhabited by some poor Negro family or run-down white. More often I would detect one as a low wing or back building of a fine house of weathered stone, a century old at least, but evidently much younger than the cabin, which, so the farmer would tell me, was his ancestor's first house. Not knowing the curious history of the log cabin, I associated these crumbling remainders with Indian wars and sieges in the wilderness, in this being quite wrong, for no notable deeds of Indian violence were committed on the Brandywine.

The country at large has been quite as ignorant as I was of the history of the architectural type which is most perfectly adapted to the settlement of a forest country, and which is more responsible than any other item, except draft beasts and the abundance of wild game, for the rapid advance of the frontier across the thousand-mile forest of primitive America back of the seaboard.

Thanks to European books on the log buildings of Finns, Scandinavians, and Russians, and thanks to a recent study of the log cabin in America,[1] it is now possible to substitute facts for this ignorance. The log cabin, which became such a powerful folk symbol in our politics and represents the coming to power of the West in this nation, began at the mouth of the Brandywine, and was not Americanized for over a century.

I shall not here go into Mr. Shurtleff's description of the various methods of building houses which the English and French brought to America. They first built rude shelters imitating the Indian wigwams; then, with sawn timber, constructed framed wooden houses, intended to be like those at home. Such houses required planks and carpenters and, unless well built, were cold and drafty in the extreme. They were beyond the competence of a pioneer moving westward

[1] *The Log Cabin Myth*, by Harold R. Shurtleff. Cambridge, 1939.

into the forest. When the English did use logs, they upended them in stockade form, and made a bad house that way. All seventeenth century pictures or reconstructions of settlements of log cabins in Virginia or New England, or anywhere in the colonies except in the Delaware valley, are quite unhistorical. One reason for the healthy toughness of the Swedes, as described by William Penn when he arrived on the Delaware, was that they did not have to live in the leaky, drafty houses which were the best, with the rare exception of a rich man's establishment near a port, which the English settlers could provide.

The Swedes, arriving with a few Finns in 1638, came from a forested region in which the typical country dwelling was constructed of log walls, the logs sometimes round, sometimes squared, with ingenious notching at the ends to make the corners tight. If the timber was pine, and the logs light, it was easy to lift them unsquared into position. If, as was the case in the great forests the Swedes found on the Delaware, the available trees were likely to be hardwood and heavy, the logs could be split, roughly squared, and then placed. The result was a house which one man, working with the simplest tools, could prepare and, with the assistance of a few strong arms, lift into place. Roofing with logs or staves, which were covered with bark, thatch, or shingle, presented no great difficulty. When completed, the builder could chop out space for his windows, and calk the interstices of his logs. Here, then, was a house type for which the materials were at hand in every wood lot, which could be easily erected in the wilderness, and which was tight, warm, dry, and durable. I follow Mr. Shurtleff in quoting from the Journal of Jasper Danckaerts, a Dutchman who traveled through the colonies in 1679-1680. Of the English-built houses in which he had the misfortune to stay on cold, windy nights, he wrote that "the dwellings are so wretchedly built, that if you are not so close to the fire as almost to burn yourself, you cannot keep warm, for the wind blows through them everywhere." But when he spent a night in Jacob Hendrix's house, near Burlington, which was built "according to the Swedish mode," he found this log hut, which was built of entire trees split through the middle, and erected without nail or spike, "very tight and warm."

On the Brandywine, the little settlement of Christinaham near the mouth was, of course, built of logs in the Swedish mode, and Governor Rising's later residence on Timber Island must also have been of log construction, probably with some of the refinements and extensions still to be seen in contemporary log houses in Scandinavia. As the Swedes

spread slowly back from the great river and up
through the highlands of the Brandywine, they built
their log cabins in each new clearing; and it is probable that the relics I knew in my youth were not built
by the Quaker ancestors who settled on those farms,
but by some Swedish predecessor. For curiously
enough, unless one considers the intense conservatism
in modes of life of the seventeenth century immigrant, the English took at least half a century before
they learned to use the highly adaptable log cabin instead of their own construction, which, in the absence
of skilled builders, was sure to be makeshift. In spite
of the fact that new settlers from the Black Forest of
Germany and from Switzerland brought with them
the log cabin idea as they, also, had practiced it at
home, it was not until the eighteenth century that
the log cabin became an American institution. Then
the new flood of immigrants, Scotch-Irish many of
them, pouring through the eastern coastland and on
into the heavily timbered Appalachians, took with
them from the Delaware the knowledge of how to
build a good house in the wilderness. By the early
nineteenth century, when the lands across the mountains were being won, it was the universal dwelling
of that new West which produced Jackson, Lincoln,
and democracy.

I had supposed, before I began to investigate the

history of these little old dwellings which were so
familiar in the Brandywine country in my youth,
that the log cabin was a fort in the wilderness, built
heavily for defense against fire, arrows, and rifle bul-
lets. That was one of its merits, but only a by-prod-
uct in its usefulness. On the Brandywine, it was no
more than the kind of house a Swede naturally built,
made easy to build by the abundance of straight timber. But when adapted by the westward moving pioneers, it became the white man's igloo, not buildable,
to be sure, in a day, but so well suited to the needs and
capabilities of a man with an ax in a forest that, like
the Eskimo, he could settle and live where, before,
comfortable living was impossible. His range was in-
definitely extended; he could stay white in his habits,
and not, like the thousands of pioneers who went over
to the Indians, turn savage in order to stay alive in
the wilderness. In that unprecedented march across a
continent which is one of the great histories of modern times, the log cabin of New Sweden, the ax, the
rifle, and Indian corn were the companions of the
pioneer.

CHAPTER SIX

Power

THE Brandywine is an unruly stream. Nowhere does it flow through a plain. Everywhere, except in the narrow lowland of the Great Valley, hills roll up softly or bluffs rise sharply from its water meadows. Spring—and sometimes early autumn—brings floods of turbid water that cover the meadows and roar through the gorge. The few eighteenth century records of the Brandywine before the battle at Chads Ford [1] concern the pleas of drovers and teamsters on the roads from Philadelphia to the westward for bridges to save them from the hazards of flooded fords and inadequate ferries; later, petitions from the farmers to have washed-out bridges replaced.

These frequent floods indicated the true wealth of the Brandywine, which was power, but power was waste without a civilization to use it.

By 1654 there were still only 368 whites in New Sweden, and only a few of these on the Brandywine. The broad Delaware was their street, and they lived up and down and on either side of it. It is quite certain that not one of them lived on the Brandywine out of sight of tidewater. In September of 1655, a

[1] The modern spelling is Chadds Ford, although the ford was named for John Chads.

77

little armada from New Amsterdam sailed up the
Delaware under command of Peter Stuyvesant. In re-
venge for the taking by the Swedes of the Dutch Fort
Casimir near where New Castle now stands, the
Dutch retook that fort, and sailed in upon Fort
Christina on the Rocks just beyond the mouth of the
Brandywine. Two of Stuyvesant's ships were an-
chored at the place where the "Fiske Kill" enters the
Christina, and of his encircling batteries one with
four companies and two guns was planted on Timber
Island between the Brandywine and the Shellpot
where I have supposed Lamberton and Turner to
have camped in 1643. This was a siege, well planned,
in good military order, and lasting fourteen days.
Lindeström, the Swedish engineer, has left an account
of the engagements decidedly more reliable than
Washington Irving's burlesque in his *Knickerbocker
History*, which has more real relation to personalities
of Jefferson's administration than to the Dutch conquest of the South River.

And so Christinaham and the Brandywine fell
into the control of the Dutch, who moved the administration of the province to Fort Casimir. But
while the Dutch owned the river, the Swedes remained where they had settled, which was chiefly
north of the Christina. If any white man lived on
the Brandywine before the 1680's he was quite cer-

tainly a Finn or a Swede, and after 1657 would have
been a subject of the city of Amsterdam in Holland,
to which the district was sold by the "Noble Lords,
Directors, Masters and Patroons" who had possessed
it. The territory went "so far landward as the boundaries of the Minquas country, with all streams, kills,
creeks, etc." belonging thereto, which included certainly all of the Brandywine. And then in 1664, New
Amsterdam having fallen, the English attacked Fort
Casimir and New Amstel (later New Castle) below
it; the commander, d'Hinoyossa, rashly refusing to
surrender, they took the forts and looted New Amstel
and the surrounding country. After this, the Brandywine became English, although whether its lower
waters were to belong to Maryland or to the region
later to be called Pennsylvania was not for some time
to be determined. Yet not until Philadelphia had been
built and, in the 1680's, Quaker settlers spread
through the old Dutch and Swedish lands, could the
Brandywine country be said to be English in fact.
Guilders and styvers were more used in trade than
pounds, shillings, and pence, and the language of the
countryfolk around the estuary of the rivers would
still have been Swedish.

These Swedes, as Penn records, were producing
enormous families of remarkably healthy children,
but soon the rush of English emigrants to Penn's lib-

eral colony greatly outnumbered them. The first
requisite of this new population was food, their next
shelter. For both of these they needed power.

Power meant falling water. It is difficult for a
modern to realize the importance of water power in
these earlier years of the Industrial Revolution, when
the potentiality of machinery began to exceed the
ability of man, horse, or ox power to run it efficiently;
and this was particularly true in a new country
where, in spite of a rapid growth in population, em-
ployable labor was always scarce. Planks had to be
sawed. Corn, which was the staple cereal before the
European cereals, wheat and barley, could be made
to grow in abundance in the too-rich soil, could not
be ground in stone mortars quickly enough for whites
accustomed to a full and regular diet. Usable power
was wealth. Nowhere in the colonies was there more
water power, more conveniently located, than on the
Brandywine.

The fall of the river from stream size in the
Welsh Hills to tidewater is close to a thousand feet
in about 60 miles. This fall is, of course, at first rapid,
and of too little volume to be useful. After the two
branches of the river reach the foot of the hills the
drop is quite evenly distributed and good for small
mills. But from the beginning of the gorge above
Wilmington there is a fall of 120 feet in four miles,

with a considerable volume of water, and at the foot
of this swift decline is tidewater and a harbor. It is
said that at the peak of its industrial development
there were 130 improved millsites on Brandywine
waters. The *Delaware Gazette*, a biweekly news and
literary journal of high quality, printed on January
26, 1793, a communication signed "Pennsylvania
Farmer," which shows that even before the great
powder industry of the Brandywine began, the river
power had been utilized to an extraordinary extent.
Pennsylvania Farmer was a man of vision, whose
project to link the Great Valley of Pennsylvania with
the port of Wilmington by canal was carried out
later by a railroad. He proposed a canal to be carried
some 36 miles and 430 feet of fall to tidewater. There
are already, he said, 50 merchant mills grinding wheat
and corn on the waters of the Brandywine, averaging
91,500 barrels during the six months of the year
when they run. In addition, are 1 furnace, 4 grist-
mills, 8 forges, 2 slitting mills, 4 paper mills, 3 oil
mills, 7 fulling mills, 1 snuff mill, 1 tilt hammer, all
run by Brandywine power.

In the seventeenth century, however, this great
industry was not dreamed of, and indeed, the rapid
fall, the volume, and the floods of the Brandywine
could not be controlled by the pioneers. They built
their primitive mills on contributory streams, such

as the Shellpot near Wilmington, or the cross-valley stream at Chads Ford, and let the main river alone. Near the old ford above the Great Falls at Wilmington, there was a Swedish barley mill earlier than 1687, which has been already mentioned in the fishing controversy, but this must have been a small affair. Samuel Kirks and associates seem to have bought this and built a mill of some size in 1727, the first of importance on the Brandywine. It was probably, as I have said, the dam built in preparation for this mill that stopped the runs of shad and sent the Indians to ask for redress from the Assembly. This mill was taken over by one of the owners, an ancestor of mine, Oliver Canby, about 1742 and marked the beginning of the great flour industry of the Brandywine.

These earliest mills on the river itself were still primitive. I have seen the remains of many when canoeing on the stream. Dams of any height were hard to build and easily swept away by the next flood. When the demand for ground wheat or corn made the household quern inadequate, some enterprising farmer bought land on the river at the head of one of the rapids which the steady fall of the Brandywine makes so numerous. Here, perhaps, was a ledge of rock or some natural obstacle, like the rock slide at Hagley where the two New Haveners saw the bear. It was not difficult to dig a short raceway from the pool above the rapids which would divert enough water to turn an undershot wheel geared to mill-stones in a little mill.

The next step was to heighten the pool by a rough dam of logs and rocks, and so increase the flow of water into the race. That is as far as the mechanics of most of the primitive sawmills for planks for the English who would build only that way, and grist-mills, flour mills for food, and later, forges for iron, had gone on the upper Brandywine. But Oliver Canby was, if not more enterprising, certainly more fortunate than most. His site was well chosen. The King's Road from Philadelphia to Baltimore crossed a ford above his mill before climbing the hills above the old Swedish settlement. It was a good place to buy grain and a good place to sell meal and flour. Before he died in early middle age he had built, about 1747, the seemly stone house on the wooded slope above Brandywine which now is the residence of the Episcopal bishop of Delaware.

His successors—and they were all of closely re-lated Quaker families—began to realize new possi-bilities. In Oliver's time, a rough bridge, which had been substituted for the ferry across the first tide-water pool of the Brandywine, was pulled down or washed away and a new bridge, probably a foot-bridge, built at the foot of the Great Falls. This opened a water route from just below the Canby mill to the Delaware and the sea, which, with a little improvement, admitted shallops and small schooners to the very foot of the Falls. By 1762 the old First Dam (I have often waded across its ruins) was built at the head of the last rapids, a long race dug on the western bank, and a powerful stream of river water sent to make power by weight as well as push on the overshot wheel of a mill at tidewater itself.

Soon the craggy east bank of the Brandywine was adventured by another ancestor of mine, Joseph Tatnall, that friend of Washington who said to him at the time of Valley Forge, "I cannot fight for thee, George, but I can feed thy men." I have his cherry-wood table on which Washington wrote his dispatches before the Battle of the Brandywine. Joseph Tatnall carried his eastern race successfully to the river bench above tidewater; and soon new dams were built above, larger races built, until, at the mouth of the Wilmington gorge, there were two sets of races, one above the other.

By 1764 there were eight mills on the Brandywine tidewater, four on each side. In 1769 the Assembly had to insist that the wheels should be fitted with board covers so that horses from the hinterland should not be frightened by their whirling clatter. And so great did the export trade become after the

Revolution that the legislature of Delaware State ordered the millers to grind a fair proportion of grain for local consumption with payment in kind. Big business, thus early, had begun to obsess the power owners, who forgot that their mills were public utilities and wanted to concentrate on buying for cash and selling abroad at a profit. By the time of the Revolution, twelve mills were functioning, their products shipped by water far and wide. One of these cost £2,000 to build with its race, exclusive of mill-hand labor.

The trade restrictions on the three lower counties were, for reasons to be stated later, much less rigorous than those in Philadelphia, and this also favored the development of a great overseas trade. By 1815, fourteen mills were grinding 500,000 bushels a year, one-half of the product exported. The flour exports ran up to $500,000 a year in value. Water rights on the Brandywine were very valuable and constituted important parts of many estates.

B. W. Winterbotham, an Englishman, in preparing his *View of the American United States* of 1795,[1] rode that way and describes the "charming prospect from the bridge," the millers' houses looking down

[1] *An Historical, Geographical, Commercial, and Philosophic View of the American United States, etc.,* by B. W. Winterbotham. London, 1795.

on the scurrying races above, the busy mills and lading ships below.

In 1789-1790, 50,000 barrels of superfine flour, 2,000 of corn meal, were ground from some 400,000 bushels of grain, and much of it exported in a fleet of small shallops from the mills, and square-riggers from the deeper waters of the Christina. It was, says Clark, in his *History of Manufactures of the United States, 1607-1860*, one of the most notable concentrations and developments of power in the colonies, which steadily increased through prosperous years up to the end of the first third of the nineteenth century.

The success of the Brandywine millers had sound reasons behind it. By the mid-eighteenth century the rich wheatlands spreading back from the Delaware and the Chesapeake were opening fast. This region of coastal plain was excellently adapted to large-scale production by means of slave labor, and soon great plantations on the Eastern Shore of Maryland and interior Delaware were growing wheat, said by Winterbotham to be of such perfection "as to be sought by the manufacturers of flour throughout the Union, and . . . preferred in foreign markets." This grain could be loaded in shallops on the many creeks and transported to the very foot of the mills themselves below the bridge on Brandywine. Joseph Tatnall bought at a single purchase the crop of an Eastern Shore planter for $40,000 cash.

The smaller hill farms of the Brandywine area were also brought into high cultivation and contributed their quota; but perhaps the most important geographical factor was the limestone region of Lancaster County, Pennsylvania, still one of the richest farming regions in America. This was the old Minquas country, and now the settlers there, following the old Minquas route, crossed a low gap in the hills and hauled their grain down to the head of navigation on the Christina for shipment by water or on to the mills direct. For this purpose they developed a heavy wagon, named Conestoga, from a region belonging to a subdivision of the Minquas tribe, which was drawn by six horses, and capable of hauling vast quantities of grain to the market in Wilmington. Sometimes twenty to thirty of these teams would be drawn up, blocking the roads, waiting to be unloaded at the mills. It was precisely this Conestoga wagon, invented to get grain to the Brandywine, that later hauled goods and families across the steep Alleghenies, and became the prairie schooner on the Santa Fe, the California, and the Oregon trails. Prairie schooner and log cabin, the two best recognized symbols of the winning of the West, both belong to the history of the Brandywine.

It can be readily seen, therefore, what an extraordinarily strategic position was held by these Brandywine mills at the Great Falls. The best grain regions in the country could reach them by easy routes for wagon or sail. Vessels carrying 1,000 to 2,000 bushels of wheat could moor at the mills, other vessels sailing from the mills themselves, or from just across the hill in the Christina, transported the flour and meal to the West Indies, whose slaves were fed from the Brandywine, from which they brought back rum and molasses, or up and down the seacoast of the United States, or to far parts of the world. It should be added that throughout this late colonial and early national period the production of flour is said to have been the most speculative of native industries. Prices for wheat fluctuated with great rapidity. The Brandywine millers had a reputation for honesty in dealings and excellence of product, but they were shrewd; they bought cheap, held, and often sold dear. The first attempt to corner wheat was made (quite successfully) by an ancestor of mine, a little later, on the Brandywine. The journals which I possess of these millers have two staples of subject matter that occupy most of their pages—religion and prices—in that order. You would scarcely know that they toiled, except on figures, were it not for an occasional item, such as "Worked all day in the race—cold."

But, thanks to the aid of mechanical invention, they were able to keep their brains on the executive side of the business.

It was on the Brandywine and in these mills that one of the early successful experiments in the co-operative standardization of a product was carried through. And it was also in these mills that perhaps the earliest example, and certainly the most successful early example, of line production anywhere was introduced. The mills, says Clarke, were abreast of and probably in advance of anything in England, which was not the case in any other American industry.

The Brandywine millers, in the time of reviving trade after the Revolution, organized a joint inspection of the products of all their mills in order to standardize the quality and weight of the flour. It was then shipped under the trade name of the Brandywine Mills, which soon became a mark of distinction, commanding the best price. By the end of the eighteenth century the American price of wheat and flour was determined on the Brandywine, as the price of steel is in Pittsburgh now. They also controlled, though I am not sure that this was co-operative among all of them, a kiln-drying process for corn meal which gave to their product unusual keeping qualities in the tropics.

But much more important and interesting were

the laborsaving processes introduced into these mills, processes so striking that Winterbotham in his report could say that three-fourths of the manual labor hitherto needed was dispensed with. The first technological unemployment in the United States seems to have been on the Brandywine, although no one in that day stayed unemployed long.

These inventions were due to an extraordinary American genius, who has had too little recognition in our histories. Oliver Evans, born on the Christina in Delaware, of Welsh Quaker stock, was an inventor at least a generation ahead of his time. He designed and built one of the earliest steamboats, and prophesied the railroad. Elizabeth Montgomery, in her delightful *Reminiscences of Wilmington,* frequently to be quoted in these pages, tells the story:

"On the day the cars commenced running from Wilmington . . . I met an old gentleman . . . who . . . said he remembered when a boy listening to Oliver Evans telling his father the time was not far off when it would be only a day's journey from Philadelphia to Baltimore, and that carriages would be invented to go without horses. This his father thought so preposterous he clapped him on the shoulder and said, 'Why, Oliver, I always thought thy brain was a little cracked, now I know it; farewell.'"

But it was Oliver who, though frustrated like so

many in his work with steamboats, designed and put into operation a prophetic and very profitable device for increasing the efficiency of water power. It seems to have been tried first in a mill on the Red Clay Creek, but it was on the Brandywine that it was perfected and reached its great usefulness. Winterbotham was immensely impressed by its success, and from his description the traditional accounts can be authenticated. From a Conestoga wagon standing by the mill or from a shallop moored in the river below the mill, the wheat was picked up mechanically, elevated to the top of the mill, cleaned as it went to the hopper, ground into flour, conveyed by screen transmission and a second series of elevators to the top of the mill again, cooled and bolted during descent, barreled, and deposited on the deck of the vessel ready for export. In all this line operation human hands were used only to fasten the tops of the barrels! This may have been, says Clarke, the first instance of uninterrupted process of mechanical manufacture from raw to finished product. Six men, employed chiefly in closing barrels, could grind annually 100,000 bushels. Evans did not get rich from his invention, though he escaped the hardships of most American inventors. The millers, however, with wheat flowing in and flour flowing out and the steady and powerful flow of the lower Brandywine made so astonishingly effective, did very well, indeed.

By the time of the Revolutionary War, these mills were already so extensive as to constitute a military factor of importance. When General Howe landed unexpectedly at the head of Elk River preparatory to the Battle of the Brandywine, there was no time, apparently, to dismantle the mills. But after he had taken Philadelphia and was settling down for the winter, with the American army watching him from near by, Washington wrote to General Potter from his headquarters (October 31, 1777) ordering the removal of the stones from the Brandywine mills. The stones were to be marked with tar or grease so as to be redistributed properly after the danger was passed. Tory, nonbelligerent, or patriot, the millers were to be spared the temptation to sell flour to the British army.

The journal of my great-great-grandfather, an undeviating Quaker, and one of these millers, is in my possession, and one volume covers most of this Revolutionary period. He was probably a believer in independence for the colonies, but he allows no expression of sympathy with either belligerent to get into his daybook. War was abhorrent to him. But one does find a distressing record of mounting prices in a currency so uncertain in value as to threaten both buyer and seller. And also his notes on transactions where, with scrupulous honesty, he carried out contracts according to real worth.

The prosperity and dominance of the Brandy-wine Mills lasted well into the first half of the nineteenth century. As late as 1834, the union formed by their coopers marched in black coats and white pantaloons when Lafayette visited Wilmington, and flour was still the town's chief industry. Nor was it the introduction of steam engines into mills that ended the first national triumph of Brandywine water power. It was the Erie Canal and the railroads, which brought into competition the vast wheatfields of the west, and particularly flour ground by a greater water power in a wider land—the falls of the Mississippi in Minnesota.

CHAPTER SEVEN

Brandywine Idyll

THE steam industry of the later nineteenth century smeared every natural beauty it touched with smoke, dirt, and waste. This was not true of water power. The capture of the swift currents of the Brandywine for work and profit was more like a seduction than a rape. The mills on its banks, the raceways on its margins, humanized nature in the eighteenth century way, changing the romance of the primitive into the sentiment of rural beauty. Not that the Brandywine was romantic to Swedes, Dutch, or Indians, or to the spiritually disciplined Quakers of the seventeenth century. Such an emotion was as foreign to them as intellectual speculation. They saw fish, game, land, power. It was not until the romantic novelists of the nineteenth century began to write of the Brandywine that crags, caves, solitude, and melodramatic beauty began to be observed by travelers to the river made famous by a battle.

Sentiment preceded romance in the United States. Irving wrote before Cooper, Poe, and Hawthorne. And, by a happy timing, the humanizing of the Brandywine made it sentimentally beautiful just when the tensities of the age of settlement relaxed into sentimental appreciation of the amenities of nature and of life. Documents, fortunately, are available for this somewhat metaphysical statement, but for one born toward the close of the age of sentiment evidence enough is still visible on the Brandywine.

There is no better way to give a touch of the idyllic to a river than to build dams, weirs, and races on its currents. Lovers of rural England have each their favorite mill, its quiet pool above in the rushes, its foaming weir, its mossy gates. But in England the mill sits usually on its little river, and seems to absorb it. The racing Brandywine, with its floods, required a different method. The builders there, whether of rock piles at the heads of rapids or of breast dams across the stream, led their races along banks and, when the fall was great, had to dig them through steep rock and usually forest, until there was enough head of water to turn a wheel and space to build the mill. Several such mills still shake their hoppers and suck in their race streams on the middle Brandywine. But everywhere, except in such slow reaches as the Lenape meadowland, there are ruined remains of dozens more, which have gone back to nature, the mill to brushy foundations, the race to a grass-lined brook or a dry bed grown with forest trees.

Such an empty trough of a water lane can be seen near Point Lookout. The tradition is that this was built by Hessian deserters, secure, so they thought, in the back country. But when Howe marched up from Maryland to take position by Chads Ford, the miller saw his opportunity, rode a lathered horse into the construction camp shouting "The British are coming," and got rid of his workers before payday.

Most of these old races have no history and are interesting enough without it. The outer rim is a pleasant walk rising higher and higher above the river, which glints and swirls between the trunks of old trees and the branches of dogwood and azalea, blooming in spring. The race itself will be feeble now, a trickle only but enough to make the race margins gardens of fern and wildflowers. There will be a waterfall down to the river through the breach of the old racegate, just before you reach the ruins of the mill.

Equally beautiful, and rich in sentiment, are the long curving dead waters above the dams, so old that their banks are as natural as the rims of mountain lakes. I should particularly recommend the mile or so above Rockland dam, soft meadows on one side rising into little hills like women's breasts, old willows on the other with deep grass beneath them, and behind, a high and rocky forest. Down this stretch the paddler, after the brief excitements of many rapids, strokes quietly in a green landscape where cattle move slowly from turf to turf, and a house of stone, orange in the evening light, waits upon time.

It is difficult to arouse such archaic sentiment now on the lower Brandywine, except by the ruined powder mills in the deep forested gorge at Hagley. The canyon at its Wilmington end is all park today, still carrying its ancient trees, but tidied, cemented, and cut by roads. Its charm is gone, though not its beauty. Yet this whole valley was famous for its sentimental beauty in the early nineteenth century. In the winding gorge, the mills for paper, textiles, and powder which used higher up the power which the flour mills below had first developed, were patriarchal, almost feudal, in their organizations. Along the banks under sycamores, oaks, and willows, and up the forested slopes on curving lanes, were (and still are) clusters of gray-stone or yellow-washed cottages, appurtenances of the mill below, making little villages—Rising Sun, Kentmere, Henry Clay, Rockland—in a quite idyllic setting, whose inhabitants were tenants of the millowner in his stone house on the upper terrace of the hill.

But the chief beauty spot was at the village of Brandywine, where the bridge crossed below the Great Falls and divided the mills and their ships on the tidewater pool from the bucolic region above where rapids ran and the millowners lived in a domestic paradise. Let Betsy Montgomery have the first word. She is describing the racewalk that led to this enchanted valley:

"A mammoth willow graces the entrance, and more than fifty years have passed since the French residents built bath-houses over the stream. . . . They also had benches placed in this race, where the servant women stood in the water to wash clothes, drying them on the grass, and we will remember the snowy whiteness of their linen . . . Here are four races, two on each end of the creek, one far above the other. That stream flowing so gently beneath, at times . . . like a furious torrent sweeps everything before it . . . Early in June it displays all its loveliness . . . the forest trees are dressed in their full verdure . . . the water falling over the dams and sprinkling its sprays around, dashing and foaming through the flood-gates like mineral waters sparkling with fixed air; whole schools of young people of every age are skipping along the banks, . . . fancifully decorating their heads with wild flowers . . . Here let us pause. Shall we not present our offering to the Lord? and meditate his works."

Elizabeth was a sentimental old lady, and my prospective great-grandmother, a Quaker heiress who came visiting "Brandywine" (the name of our family house) with her sister in 1800 was more romantic if no less sentimental. Her unpublished Journal is mislaid and I cannot, as I wished, quote from her direct. But I have read her description of an early evening on the lower Brandywine many times. With her companions she floats on the Barley Mill Dam, while the last birds are singing and from the cabin of Alexander Rohan, the romantic exile, come the plaintive notes of a flute. The river paused for them before it rushed down to the mills. To be sure, she was in love!

The earliest large-scale industry in the United States had touched the Brandywine with a kindly hand. The mills themselves were well below the mouth of the valley. Behind them on the northern bank was the highly picturesque village of Brandywine, some of whose quaint houses still remain.[1] On the southern bank, the outlying houses of Wilmington began with quaint brick homes of early Quakers and Swedes. It was a long walk to Wilmington itself, up Brandywine Walk shaded by sycamores, over a forested hill, and down to the town which still kept close to the Christina. But above the bridge, where the overflow of the races poured in steep cataracts down either bank, the narrow wooded valley had become a Quaker idyll. I can remember vividly from my youth the scene when only a steel bridge and a

[1] The illustration facing page 156 is of an old Quaker lyceum and library, still standing in Brandywine village.

dirt road had been added to the scene. On the south bank was "Brandywine," where four generations of us had lived. It was an ample, decorous house of brick, standing above its gardens which sloped down into shrubbery above the grassy edge of the first race; then down again under forest trees and on a slope famous for wildflowers to the rocks and roaring rapids of the Falls. Upstream a little was Oliver Canby's house, built about 1747, and rebuilt after three wagonloads of Dupont powder had blown its front down. I have a child's painting of it as it was about 1800, called "Mr. Canby's Mansion on Brandywine." It was stuccoed or whitewashed over stone then, and looked, rather severely, on a little formal garden, perched on the woody edge of the race, a bathhouse at one side, and then the steep slope through the woods to the river.

Across the Brandywine, the Tatnalls, Prices, and Leas—millers all—had built their Quaker houses of gray cut stone above the village highway, the most southerly overlooking the rock wall from which the upper race had been cut and within hearing of the fall which in times of high water splashed down into the Brandywine.

And between these gardened homes the river, when I was a boy, still ran as wild as ever. Men swung suspended nets for suckers below the falls of dam or rapid, forest birds nested in the undergrowth, and a child wandering there could still believe himself on a primitive river though only a few hundred yards away from streets and homes.

CHAPTER EIGHT

Emigré Capital

THE happy combination of power in great quantity delivered by the useful Brandywine at what was, in effect, an arm of the sea, brought wealth to the town of Wilmington and the village of Brandywine, made ports of them, might have made them great ports if the channels had been deeper. And this wealth, whose foundation was Brandywine flour, attracted ambitious men. Then, by a fall of the cards of circumstance, the firm high lands between the Christina and the Brandywine, already prosperous, livable, and accessible from abroad, became the scene for a little while of a brilliant and cosmopolitan society. It will not be departing from the history of a river to describe the flowering of this early community of émigrés, for they came to a town made comfortable by the Brandywine's contribution to economic stability, sailed many of them direct to its estuary, and remained, some of them at least, to bring Brandywine power to its peak of production.

Evanescent as a dream, this Wilmington and Brandywine society of the turn of the eighteenth into the nineteenth century, exists only in legend and in memory, and awaits a novelist to make its charm and strange contrasts live again in the imagination.

It flourished between two wars, but struck down no roots, and lived on after the repatriations at the end of the Napoleonic era only in the social life of the du Pont dynasty, and in the guiding traditions of half a dozen Delaware families, who kept large views in a small state and exercised a leadership in the nation out of proportion to the size of the community from which they came.

When the Swedes built Christinaham, they hoped to ship from there furs, to make them rich, and other products of the New World. For this purpose, and for any kind of trade, the site seemed well chosen. But, unfortunately for their expectations, the later settlement at Philadelphia, on the Delaware itself, with ample wharf room and land routes to the West, became too strong a competitor for sea-borne commerce. Nor did the more southerly location of Wilmington help it to become a center of transportation. Travelers abroad, like Franklin, who wished to escape the slow and tortuous navigation of the upper Delaware, passed Wilmington, and took ship on the broad bay off New Castle. And, later, travelers came to New Castle by steamboat, crossed the narrow isthmus to the Chesapeake, and so on to the South. It was not until the great railroad age that Wilmington finally extinguished the old capital of the region.

Nevertheless, industry based on Brandywine

power gave the little town, now, in the eighteenth century, more English than Swedish, an importance of its own. Many ships were built on the deep Christina and some on the Brandywine, and these ships, with others, found ready employment in carrying kiln-dried meal and standard flour from the mills on Brandywine throughout the coasts of the colonies and abroad. The shipbuilding history of the town was to last into the twentieth century. James Hemphill, a sea captain, whose log book has been published by the Historical Society of Delaware,[1] records the shipping of flour to Havre, Antwerp, Calcutta, and Java, and the return of products from distant ports. Staves of white or red oak from the Delaware forests were shipped, too, for sugar hogsheads in the West Indies. In 1789 there were eleven ships and brigs trading to the West Indies; and seven in the Irish trade, bringing back immigrants, and Waterford glass for rich Quaker households, some of which I possess.

Christinaham changed its name to Willingtown when an English settler of that cognomen married Swedish land and began to develop a town. He failed. It must have been about 1729, just after her marriage to William Shipley of Pennsylvania, that my great-great-great-great-grandmother, Elizabeth Levis, a preacher to the Friends, dreamed of a journey

[1] No. LXIV.

through wild country, ending in a high hill from which she saw a lovely prospect of valleys, rivers, clearings, and settlers' cabins. Her guide told her that it was a new settlement which was to become populous, and that Divine Providence designed that she and her family should move thither and receive the blessings of heaven upon their labors. On awaking she told her husband, who replied that he did not expect to become an inhabitant of fairy land. But several years later, riding on a religious visit to the Friends of the Delaware peninsula, Elizabeth crossed the Brandywine on the old ford above the Great Falls, climbed the hill above it, and, coming out on a little clearing near a Swedish log cabin, saw, stretching before her, the winding creeks of Christina and Brandywine, meeting to join the Delaware, and the valleys, marshes, sloping lawns, and interspersed forests of her dream. She persuaded her skeptical husband that Providence had a hand in it; though it was not until he had seen the natural advantages of Brandywine power at tidewater that he consented to remove his family, his energy, and his wealth to the new region. Buying land in 1735, building a market house which caused a characteristically American downtown-uptown controversy, and financing both milling and trade, he was the true founder of Wilmington, which was renamed for a distinguished English family. His daughter married Oliver Canby, the first successful miller, and after his death Poole, another miller, her shrewd father having advised her that these were the two most eligible men in the community. With the impulse given, Wilmington went in for whaling and lumber as well as for flour, fortified itself against pirates, knew sea losses and sea tales. Of these the raciest is Betsy Montgomery's account of the captain given up for lost who returned on a night of storm, fell into his own well, and was first seen by his horrified wife as a dripping head, green in the flashes of lightning, emerging from underground.

Two circumstances, for which the Brandywine had no responsibility beyond its steady contribution of wealth from flour, account for the sudden change of the little community between the creeks from a provincial village to an émigré capital of the lower river region.

Delaware, before the Revolution, had been known as the Three Lower Counties on Delaware, and was part of Pennsylvania, but since 1704 these counties were really autonomous. With their Swedish and Dutch populations, they were difficult to amalgamate with Penn's government. Penn liked the Swedes, for they were good settlers and clearers of land, but both Swedes and Dutch and the new English immigrants who, in the eighteenth century,

opened up the level lands of the Peninsula, were rest-
ive under control from upriver. Their problems were
different. They were alien to the Quakers, either by
blood or by religion, for lower Delaware was predominantly Anglican, Presbyterian, or later, Metho-
dist. Geographically, upper Delaware belonged to the
Pennsylvania region, but the long-drawn-out dispute
over boundaries with Maryland left in all the lower
counties a sense of doubtful title which encouraged
a desire for self-government. Declared an independent
state in 1776, the new government in one of its first
acts lightened the commercial restrictions that had
been placed upon Pennsylvania trade, and gave the
port of Wilmington advantages which Philadelphia
did not enjoy. And it should be added that, from the
very beginning, Wilmington, though built on a rep-
lica of Philadelphia's town plan, had, like New
Castle, an independence and originality of its own in
law, trade, and the nature of its population.

That the liberalizing of commerce would have
brought much more shipping to Wilmington to add
to the carriers of grain and flour is improbable. But
now, just as the prosperity of the little town began to
attract the attention of foreigners seeking, or forced
to seek, a new home, a much more powerful stimulus
rushed ships and new inhabitants to the Christina and
the Brandywine. A devastating plague of yellow fever

settled upon Philadelphia in 1793, and again in 1795, 1796, and 1798. Wilmington escaped, was not attacked until 1798, and it was generally believed that there was a salubrity in the air of the Brandywine-Christina region which brought immunity to the disease. One supposes that, by good luck, the very imperfect quarantine kept away, for a while, any actual cases of fever from the mosquitoes of the estuary marshes. However this may have been, the result was a rush of hundreds from Philadelphia to Wilmington, including Thomas McKean, the governor. Industry followed, until the Christina "bristled" with masts, many of sea-borne ships afraid to unload upriver. Immigrants from abroad landed here instead of in Philadelphia, more grain came to the Brandywine mills, more flour went out. The quiet little town, with its brick houses overlooking the Christina, and its wooded hills across which Conestoga wagons rumbled to the mills, knew a brief experience of booming trade and overcrowded homes, and a sudden flowering of cosmopolitanism. The population of 1,200 doubled between 1776 and 1790, and doubled again by the War of 1812.

I have sketched in the economic background of these years because I am sure that Brandywine power and the capital it accumulated and the pleasant town it so largely created were the foundations for this

quite brilliant moment in Delaware history. For example, the Duc de La Rochefoucauld-Liancourt, famous American traveler, wondering in 1797 whether
the banks recently incorporated in Wilmington had
any real necessity, "except to the Brandywine millers," remarked that "the flour trade . . . [is] the
only branch of commerce that is carried on to any
extent in this state." And peppery evidence of the
importance of the mills is to be found in *Porcupine's
Gazette* (September 19, 1797), that lively journal of
political propaganda directed against French influence in the United States, and published in Philadelphia by William Cobbett, later to become a famous English publicist. Cobbett had fled to France
from England as a result of his own indiscretions, and
then to America, and, like the many wanderers to be
mentioned later, came to Wilmington where he lived
on Quaker Hill from 1792 to 1794. The Cobbett of
this period was a fiery Tory, very different from the
Conservative Liberal predecessor of Disraeli who
fought later in England for humanitarian reform,
and wrote that admirable book, *Rural Rides,* for the
improvement of English country life. In America, he
was always in hot water, which may account for the
acid tone of his story of an attempted blockade of
the Brandywine mills. A French privateer had an-
chored "off the Brandywine," presumably at its

mouth or in the near-by Delaware, and forced the
local schooner, *Flying Fish,* which seems to have been
leaving the mills with a cargo, to heave to. She succeeded in slipping off by a clever trick, but the incident released Cobbett's wrath:

"And where were the noble Wilmington battalions—those citizen soldiers, those *centaurs of lib-
erty?* . . . We hear enough of these gallant youths
on a fourth of July . . . Where were they say, when
Mounseer was blockading the Brandywine mills, and
blazing away upon their brother citizens? . . .
When one of their own merchant vessels was endeav-
oring to elude the embargo in 1794, and get off with
her cargo to a *British port,* then did their manly
bosoms burn for glory. Like true citizen soldiers, out
they scampered, rough and ready, and swore they
would fight under the banners of the constable to the
last drop of their blood. Even the *hickory Quakers*
(with which Wilmington unfortunately abounds)
rushed down through the swamps like so many swine,
to stop the criminals . . . One vessel had *cannons on
board,* the other *had none.*"

The rather extraordinary group of immigrants
that flour prosperity and yellow fever in Philadelphia
seems to have turned toward the Brandywine had
left home for reasons of their own. These late 1780's
and the 1790's were decades of violent disturbance

abroad. From France in revolution a stream of aristocrats and conservatives out of sympathy with, or in
violent danger from, the new regime, flowed into
England and the Continental nations, and then, as
their plight grew more desperate, to America to seek
new refuges or new homes. In 1791, the terrible
Negro insurrection in Santo Domingo drove out such
rich planters as were not massacred. The troubles in
Ireland contributed their quota of refugees from
British oppression, many of whom came direct to
Wilmington on ships trading from that port. And as
the Napoleonic age got under way, wars all over
Europe sent more émigrés desirous of safety or of a
new life in a more hopeful continent.

The most numerous and most gregarious of the
émigrés were French. Wilmington and New Castle
had been well advertised in French aristocratic circles by officers of the French Army assisting in our
Revolution, who were quartered there or made at
home by various families in the lengthy operations
around Philadelphia and the marches north and south.
Travelers like Rochefoucauld-Liancourt had written
of Wilmington. Lafayette, in particular, had a special
affection for the two towns on lower Delaware, and
Molly Vining, of whom more later, was a focus for
French gallantry and talked of abroad.

Whatever the causes, so many French refugees

arrived in the early days of the Revolution in France
that a street was named for them, French Street,
which runs from the Christina to the Brandywine,
and is still so called. Here they lived in rectangular
houses of brick or stone, some of which still remain,
and soon created a pleasant similitude of their old life
at home, meeting in frequent entertainments in garden or salon, and bringing to the Quaker town a
finesse of social relation, a courtesy in manner, a
sophistication, and a distinction in dress, as unfamiliar
and as unexpected as a pheasant's finery in a chicken
coop.

It was Pierre Bauduy, one of the Santo Domingo planters, who designed in 1798 the graceful
Wilmington town hall, still standing and now a museum. It was he who purchased from the Comte de
Ségur, uncle by marriage of Lafayette, Eden Park
across the Christina, which had been Robert Morris's
summer place, and put on his gateposts two rams in
masonry, in memory of the famous Don Pedro, a
merino imported from Spain. In my youth, these
rams still stood, and were said by our nursemaids to
jump down and turn around thrice when they heard
the bells of Wilmington strike twelve, a tricky saying
that puzzled us. It was with Bauduy that the first
du Pont joined to begin the powder mills on Brandywine. Others of the French were poor, like the Mar-

quise de Sourci, who lived in a cottage near French Street, supported by her son, who invented a grasshopper that skipped on the ice and built boats from one of which he was drowned. But many were well-to-do and gay. The Garesché family had a charming double garden looking down upon the marshes of Christina and out over the Delaware. In one of the gardens was an octagonal garden house, in winter a hothouse, in summer a salon, with a lattice summerhouse above for hot nights. In this society was Pierre Provenchère who had been tutor to the Duc de Berri, and his daughter who had been educated with the Princesse Royale. And probably Méchaud Martel, who taught four languages to Theodosia Burr; and certainly General Bauduy, an aide to Napoleon. There was the distinguished Alsatian chemist, John James Ullmann, pupil, like the first du Pont, of the great Lavoisier; and Colonel Ann Louis de Toussard, who lost an arm in our Revolution, and lived in a stone house, lined against the weather with canvas, on which his talented guests painted landscapes, birds, and flowers.

Louis Philippe, the Duc d'Orléans, later king of the French, was here, probably more than once, with his two brothers of the house of Orléans. From 1796 to 1800 they were in exile in the United States, while Louis watched for an opportunity to slip on to the throne. But Napoleon got ahead of him. He is reported to have taught school in Wilmington. More probably, he gave an occasional lesson in French in return for hospitality. The brothers spent lavishly in the United States, nevertheless, in 1797 they were too poor to leave Philadelphia when the yellow fever began, and no money came through until September. Perhaps Louis exchanged French then for food and lodging in some Federalist household in Wilmington, which was still free from the fever.

So teeming was the town with these immigrants, that Henry Pepper, a graduate of "Dublin College," gave lessons in English to the émigrés and in French to the natives, who felt it to be "genteel" to learn the foreign tongue. William Cobbett, who wrote his *"Le Tuteur Anglais"* (1795), for the instruction of the French refugees in Wilmington, was his assistant.

I am not writing a history of Wilmington, but only trying to picture an extraordinary society for a tiny town. Nor was the distinction of this society limited to its émigré French. Benjamin H. Latrobe, architect of part of the Washington Capitol, was a resident. So was Robert Coram, the librarian, who published a plan for a general system of education in the new United States. Hezekiah Niles, the founder of the famous *Niles Register* of Baltimore, perhaps the best known of our early newspapers, lived and worked first in Wilmington. Louis McLane, later minister to England, was a native son. On Federal Hill, so called because, for a while, the national capital was projected there, lived another native son who awaits his place in a historical novel. Dr. James Tilton, surgeon general in the War of 1812, was an utter democrat among all these aristocrats, "a sour, wry-faced incorrigible democrat," Cobbett called him most unfairly. He wore tow homespun linen to receptions at the White House, and when he lost a leg from a war injury, had a giant cradle made in which to rock himself for exercise. He chewed tobacco and served Delaware and the ladies in Congress and out of it. The first of five Bayards to sit in the United States Senate was also active in this golden day of the Christina and the Brandywine.

As early as 1773, such was the vigor of the town and its neighboring Brandywine village, that an Academy was built, with Laurence Girelius, last Swedish pastor of the old Swedes Church as president. (Parenthetically, it may be added that a brother of Emanuel Swedenborg had taught under the jurisdiction of the Swedish ecclesiastical establishment.) Here Franklin is said to have conducted an electrical experiment before its forty to fifty students, and Rush and Rittenhouse, of Philadelphia, and John Dickinson, famous for his Revolutionary pamphlets, lectured. The names of petitioners for the charter indicate the cosmopolitanism of the town even then— they include Quaker English, worldly English, French, Swedish, Dutch names. There was a Lyceum, so called, as well as an Academy, and in 1799 they were debating "Are novels profitable or pernicious to youth?"

And there were still other notable figures, émigrés or temporary residents. Of William Cobbett I have already spoken. Talleyrand must have been a visitor from Philadelphia, though there is no record. General Lewis Cass, on his way to the West and a reputation, taught school. So did John Filson, first historian of Kentucky, who, after being captured by the Indians, returned to Wilmington to get his book published by James Adams, the local printer.

But the most engaging of all the exiles lived on the Brandywine itself in a cabin in a meadow just above the Falls. He has already been mentioned in the passage cited from Elizabeth Canby's Journal. Alexander Hamilton Rowan (1751-1834) was heir to Killyleagh Castle in County Down, Ireland. He was a singularly handsome man, whose memorable part in Irish revolutionary history was owing to his birth, wealth, and willingness to fight anyone for a good cause rather than to any fervid radicalism. He would be forgotten in general history except for a famous

speech delivered by Curran, the Irish orator and patriot, at his trial. In his youth, he had been rusticated
from Cambridge for throwing a tutor into the Cam.
He joined the army, became celebrated in Ireland for
his defence of a girl who had been seduced and then
double-crossed afterward, and later, meeting the
celebrated rebel, Wolfe Tone, was persuaded to join
the Society of United Irishmen. His function was to
call out any member of the Dublin Parliament who
spoke disrespectfully of the society, but when he
crossed to Scotland to challenge the lord advocate,
he was judged to be a dangerous man and arrested
on the false charge of circulating a seditious pam-
phlet. The government apparently intended to hang
him, but he escaped by bribing his jailer, got to France
with £2,000 reward on his head, was there intimate
with Mary Wollstonecraft, mother of Mary Shelley,
came to Philadelphia on July 18, 1795, and within
three days, was one of the leaders of a mob which
tried to overawe Washington into rejecting the Jay
treaty.

Wilmington seemed a good retreat. He settled
there, first in relative poverty, which was soon relieved. Out of bravado, or necessity, he sold birch beer
on the street from a barrow and worked as a gardener.

When money came he opened a calico mill at the
dam near the old ford on the Brandywine, which in

1799, when his friends were arranging to end his exile, he offered for sale in the *Delaware Gazette*. When there were no takers, he inserted a final advertisement of unusual honesty: "Any person inclining to sacrifice his property by carrying on this manufactory in America, may have the whole for one half of the sum they cost"! It went by auction. Rowan was visited by the Irish rebels Tandy and Tone, but he had seen real revolution in France and preferred even calico to intrigue. Two dogs, named for his faraway children, a flute, and a good library were his companions. And so this duelist, eccentric, and romantic rebel lived for five years on his Brandywine meadow in friendly intercourse with his Quaker neighbors of the mills, one of whom became his intimate friend. By 1800 the troubles in Ireland had subsided, and he was allowed to return and enter into his estate again. It was to Rowan that Shelley went first when he visited Ireland, but probably found the man more sympathetic than his principles.

Perhaps the best evidence of the cosmopolitanism of Wilmington at the end of the eighteenth century is the striking story of Mary Vining. Born in Delaware in 1756, dying in 1821, rich, extraordinarily beautiful, she was a bluestocking of the order of those remarkable women who conducted the salons of Paris, only more beautiful than most though equally accomplished. She was known at the time of our Revolution as a wit and a beauty throughout three armies, and had admirers in all. The unfortunate André penciled a miniature portrait of her, a copy of which is preserved. Lafayette was her close friend and lifelong correspondent. His descriptions of her charm, and the compliments of that ami of Marie Antoinette, the Comte de Fersen, aroused the curiosity of the queen, who asked Jefferson for a description, and is said to have invited her to Versailles. LaRochefoucauld-Liancourt and the Duc d'Orléans were her visitors. Anthony Wayne heard of her wit through Lafayette, was brought to call from his headquarters at Joseph Tatnall's on Brandywine to her house in Wilmington, and fell in love in spite of his vivacious wife at home. She spoke French fluently, gave herself to no man until the tragic sequel, because, as she said, the admiration of one man was not enough. She was said by the gossip, Betsy Montgomery, to have had a coquetry of never exposing all her face at once—a fan, a veil, a scarf, hid always some of her lovely features.[1] She was cousin of Caesar Rodney, hero of the ride to place the last-needed signature on the Declaration of Independence. He had loved her beautiful

---

[1] Debunking historians say that this was a trick of age when she had lost her teeth. I repel such a disillusioning suggestion, which has no better evidence than Betsy's tradition.

aunt, also called Molly, and for him she often acted as hostess in Wilmington.

When she was thirty-nine, and still beautiful, Wayne, now the hero of Fallen Timbers and a widower, met her again in Philadelphia and fell once more. This time it was a whirlwind courtship, spreading scandal down the Peninsula where her relatives lived, for he stayed in her house with only servants present. It is quite possible that they were lovers. Their engagement was announced; he sent her a Lowestoft set; they bought furniture for a house in New Castle. Then Washington sent Wayne to arrange for taking over the western British forts after the signing of Jay's treaty, and to negotiate with the Indians. He died in the wilderness of what seems to have been appendicitis. After his death she retired to a little cottage called the Willows, near where Brandywine Walk reached the Kennett turnpike.

Her brother, a child of fortune, died after impoverishing the family, leaving four children to her guardianship. In order to place the youngest she made what tradition describes as a sensational reappearance from obscurity in Philadelphia society, wrote a part at least of a history of the Revolution, which was unfortunately burned by accident, and died in seclusion. "Six ladies," I quote from Elizabeth Montgomery, "with about three yards of white linen drawn

over the bonnet tied under the chin hung loose,"
were mourners at her funeral. Her forehead, even in
death, was "incomparable."

And so the great world outside sent its exiles
for a while to a provincial little town, which, after
the restoration at the end of the Napoleonic era, soon
became provincial again, and lived a quietish nineteenth century life where Quakerism and the Industrial Revolution were far more influential than
French manners and European ideas. I have tried to
describe its quality toward the end of the century,
and just before big business and great wealth made
it a modern capital of finance, in a book called *The
Age of Confidence*. Yet, if I had a chance to run
back on the time stream of Brandywine history I
would choose to stop in the 1790's, and preferably at
the lower end of Brandywine Walk. There, before
steamboat days, the flow of distinguished travelers
north and south crossed the creek by bridge or ferry.
Washington in his coach was ferried again and again
at the foot of French Street, with some difficulty for
the coach was large. French generals, southern states-
men, George Whitefield, the famous English preacher
(but he would have come earlier) who preached to
three thousand under the oaks on Academy Hill,
Aaron Burr "in his coach drawn by four black
horses," Lafayette after a call on Molly Vining, and

again as an old man leaning to pat the head of the grandchild of his old friend Joseph Tatnall—the children on the banks must have had plenty to watch.

But what makes this brief period fascinating to a social historian is the sharp contrast between the gay society of émigrés, Federalist aristocrats, or distinguished travelers and the plain Quaker background against which they moved. For it was the Quakers, their Brandywine power, and their trade which contributed much of the character and even more of the economic stiffening of the community.

The Quakers were spiritual radicals in a country already intensely competitive and eager to get rich rapidly. Their religion went deep with them, and while it did not prevent them from becoming wealthy, it strongly disciplined the shows, the vanities, the frivolities, and the vice which accompanied wealth and obscured the spiritual operations of the inner light. Inside their meetings, where both men and women spoke, there was constant testimony against worldliness, and outside they were eager pamphleteers and propagandists, traveling, like Elizabeth Levis, up and down the land to strengthen the morale of their Society of Friends. Straight-spoken, calling all men and women by their first names, accustomed to challenge, and meek only in physical violence, they must have been tough arguers. No respect for royalty weakened their general tendency toward republican principles. In later years, William Cobbett said that "he had lived in the hotbed of democracy, on Quaker Hill [in Wilmington] amid the Stars, whose political horizon was so brilliant, he scarcely dare defend royalty."

The trading Quakers lived chiefly on this Quaker Hill, an eminence above the Christina, where their meetinghouse, a square brick building with a truncated roof sheltering the doorway, stood in great simplicity. It was surrounded by solid brick houses, many well designed, as substantial as the Friends that owned them. The Quaker millers lived in the lovely valley of Brandywine village. All were still a "peculiar people." Gray or brown in dress, the men wore low, broad-brimmed hats, the women scuttle bonnets, their clothes plain but, where there was wealth, of the finest material. They still said *thou* and *thy*, not *thee* and *thy*. They were abolitionists, temperance advocates, enemies of extravagance, of waste, and of war. Except for excellent taste in household furnishings, they were unaesthetic in principle and in practice, but unworldliness did not preclude hardheaded business, unless it was dishonest or profited by slavery or war. The best Quaker consciences were nice. David Ferris, ancestor of the first historian of the river settlements, refused to take his share of the profits of a West India trade, because they were too great to be justifiable. In spite of such scruples, the Quakers prospered more than their neighbors. A combination of thrift, energy, and simplicity of living is unbeatable. And there were no poor Quakers. If poverty was due to misfortune, the meeting relieved it; if to character, the man was not a real Quaker.

What a contrast in dress, customs, ideas, temperaments, and philosophies of life could have been seen on Brandywine Walk on a Sunday morning! The collarless coats and deep bonnets of the Quakers walking home from meeting; farmers from the country still dressed in clothes, as we are reliably informed, of the old Swedish patterns; a Reade or a Rodney on horseback up from New Castle; and French aristocrats in finery, faded a little perhaps but jauntily worn, on their way to their bathhouses on the race. How the simple must have stared! And even Elizabeth Montgomery, an Anglican not averse to worldliness, though sure that most pleasures were followed by calamity, was overcome with astonishment at the court dress worn in her youth by the nine- or ten-year-old son of Girelius, the aforesaid last of the Swedish ministers, a man of station in his own country.

"His long flaxen hair was powdered, cued, and tied with a black ribbon. A ruffled shirt and cambric stock plaited fine, fastened behind with a buckle set with stone; buff vest and breeches; knee and shoe-buckles set, white silk stockings and black slippers, the buckles of which covered the whole instep; a long-tailed coat of either scarlet or blue broadcloth, and a three-cornered cocked-hat; a gold-headed cane."

If they dressed thus in the French salons at the court end of the town, the "hickory" Quakers must often have expected to meet the Scarlet Woman of Babylon on their quiet streets.

CHAPTER NINE

More Power and the du Ponts

THE granite gorge of the Brandywine, that falls with rapid after rapid for four miles to tidewater, provides the climax of the river's power. In the eighteenth century, when the raw materials for manufacture and the products to be shipped were heavy, and transportation on land was difficult, the power just above tidewater and access to deep water was, naturally, in greatest demand. But with the building of, first, roads, and then railroads, the still more abundant power in the curving canyon above Wilmington attracted hard-working men. Before steam ended the water power age in the mid-nineteenth century (to be revived, of course, with electricity), the river from Rockland to its estuary presented, in mills of many varieties, an illustrated history of industrial economics. At one time or another, nearly every mill product of the America of that time was made on the Brandywine; but four industries dominated, and one, beginning there in its first successful manufacture in America, became of international importance. As the price of wheat for the country was set by the flour mills on the Brandywine, so, later, the price of gunpowder was to be fixed by the powder mills of the du Ponts. The two other important uses of the Brandywine were for textile making and for paper.

As early as 1787, Joshua and Thomas Gilpin had begun the manufacture of paper on the Brandywine in the gorge above Wilmington. In 1816 they patented, and in 1817 put into operation at their plant at Kentmere, a machine for producing a continuous roll of paper instead of the single sheets of earlier manufacture. An old woodcut of the mills shows a high stone building on a sweeping curve of the river against a background of terraces and forest and cottages tucked in the trees. Industrialism has always touched the Brandywine valley with a gentle hand.

On Gilpin paper, watermarked "Brandywine," newspapers, such as the *Delaware Gazette,* were soon printed, and its excellence and cheapness made possible the expansion of book publishing which took place in Philadelphia about that time. Such ambitious undertakings as the reprinting of Lavoisne's atlas now became practicable. The Gilpin patent, however, was quickly infringed by not too scrupulous New Englanders, and the freshets of the Brandywine—especially the great flood of 1839—and a fire ended their prosperity. But papermaking, at the Augustine mills above the stone-arched bridge of the Baltimore & Ohio Railroad and at Rockland, still continues.

Another Delawarean, Jacob Broom, moved his cotton-spinning plant in 1795 to the Brandywine in order to get power, and established what is said to have been the first real cotton factory in the United States. In 1824, Joseph Bancroft, who had been apprenticed to the father of John Bright, the English Quaker statesman, arrived in Delaware to join John Bancroft, who had a small woolen mill at the foot of the Great Falls. In 1831, Joseph took over the power where the paper mills were still operating, and began a cotton-milling business which expanded until now it is of national importance. There was a 22-foot fall at the milldam, which gave power enough until 1858 —and some idea of the strength of Brandywine water. It was with special reference to the cotton mills that the first attempt to safeguard the interests of child labor is recorded for Delaware. An Association for the Encouragement of Manufactures had been chartered, which proposed that working children should be allowed time off for education, but cautiously compromised with the rights of capital by suggesting that millowners be paid for the time lost in school!

The Quaker grain millers, the du Ponts, and the Bancrofts were the three lasting dynasties of industrialists on the lower Brandywine, although, by the time of the rise to national prominence of textiles and powder, Brandywine flour was rapidly declining. Joseph Bancroft's two sons, William and Samuel, illustrated once more the curious contrasts in mores which have been so characteristic of the Wilmington region. William was a strict Friend in the years when the discipline of the meeting had become a legend or a byword. He sat on the elder's bench when I, as a child in the Friends' School, attended Fifth-day meeting, and while he seldom spoke, he looked example. Living simply, dressing plainly, he did good. When he died he left in trust for posterity a stretch of wild Brandywine bank and valley, beginning just above the du Pont holdings and stretching up the east shore and over the hills above it, to the Pennsylvania line—a noble area of park in which it was his hope that men and women loving nature and simplicity of living would be enabled to afford homes in an unspoiled countryside. The land is there and the river, still unspoiled and safe from exploitation, but the trustees have been uncertain as to how to fulfill his dream.

The other son, Samuel, in violent reversion from Quakerism, fell in love with sensuous beauty, and made a great collection of pre-Raphaelite paintings, now trusteed for the city of Wilmington. It was Rossetti's Fiametta that first inflamed his imagination. What his Quaker father would have thought of that symbol of spiritual sensuality, it is impossible to say!

Above Kentmere, the industrialized district of the Brandywine once extended on one bank or the other as far as Rockland. Yet, as I have said in a previous chapter on the idyllics of the Brandywine, the romantic canyon was humanized but never made ugly. The picturesque wildness of cliff and slope and forest within Wilmington city limits and above the Brandywine park, which Elizabeth Montgomery describes as abounding in copperheads and rattlesnakes, is, to be sure, scarred by deep quarries of blue granite, begun for the building of the Delaware breakwater off Lewes in 1828. In my youth the overhill road from the Brandywine quarries to the town was the place to watch for the quarry teams, three heavy horses in tandem, jingling with brass ornaments, driven by a dusty-faced darky, and hauling a great slab of granite, suspended by chains from a long four-wheeled truck. But above the quarries and the textile and paper mills, the river is heavy forest on one side—the remains of the ancient Alapocus Forest of the Indians—with ancient mills, some ruined, while on the other are the rows of workmen's cottages of yellow-splashed brown-rusted stone, white silled and doored, running beside the water or up the hills. No through road goes up this river. You must drive down from the highlands on the old mill roads to reach it. Breck's Mill, once Victor du Pont's woolen mill, is at the end of one of these roads. That was a dancing place for the du Pont tribe in my time, where, between dances, couples hung out the windows to watch the moonlight on the roaring water over the dam.

A little above Rising Sun, on the lands where Jacob Broom spun cotton goods, the du Pont family began in 1802 a modest manufacture of gunpowder which became, under the name of The Dupont Company (notice the difference of spelling), probably the greatest chemical industry in the world. The history of this company is one of the most striking and significant stories in American industrial history, with social aspects of great interest also. In six generations of family control, this history spans the economics of the power-machine age, from its naïve beginnings to the present.

Pierre Samuel Dupont (1739-1817) was the son of a French watchmaker and trained as such. But under the influence of his mother, he studied, and emerged as an intellectual and a pamphleteer in those decades of financial and political disturbance which preceded the French Revolution. Economics—the economics of trade and of agriculture—was his field, and he was fortunate in catching the attention of Turgot, Louis XVI's able minister, and eventually in becoming his valued assistant. As state official and as editor of liberal magazines, he established his fortune and made such a reputation that he was sent to Poland as tutor for the young prince. Recalled by Turgot, he was caught and nearly ruined by the uncertainties of the times—a fate which was to occur in series for the rest of his life. A physiocrat, friend to Franklin, acceptable at court, a liberal but a monarchist, he was a type example of the enlightened French intellectual of the age when French thinking was leading the world.

He had two sons—one handsome, social, cultivated, and a visionary; the other slow, a hard worker, who managed the printing business of his father, and was given an opportunity to study chemistry under Lavoisier, and to work in the government mills under his supervision.

Victor, the handsome and diplomatic, was sent to America in the train of the French minister, where he made good connections in Federalist circles and got about the country. Later, he returned, and was made consul general during the French troubles, but not accepted by President Adams. Pierre Samuel just escaped the guillotine, but was unable to win favor with the Directoire. By this time he had been ennobled, called himself du Pont, and added de Nemours from the town which he had represented in the Assembly. With an uncertain future in France, and inspired by accounts of America from our Robert Fulton, and trusting to Victor's knowledge of the new country and his own friendship with Jefferson, he decided to remove the whole family to America, and seek new fortunes there.

The plan was characteristic of an intellectual and an optimist. The du Ponts were to establish a promoting and trading agency to deal in everything profitable from land to exchange. Stock was sold in the enterprise, and soon they were in America. It was fortunate that the second brother, Eleuthère Irénée, went along. While Victor endeavored to make a fortune in supplying Napoleon's Santo Domingo army, the plodding Irénée sought for power and a good location for a powder mill. The crash that brought down the airy speculations of Du Pont de Nemours, Père, Fils & Cie. of New York, left the powder business as the only assets of the enterprise.

Irénée was impressed by the power available on the Brandywine, and the excellent location between Washington, Baltimore, Philadelphia, and New York. He bought the Broom property of 75 acres and some buildings, halfway up the Brandywine gorge. There he worked furiously, burdened with debt. Machinery was made in France for him, and the French government, willing to help competition with what was, in effect, an English monopoly, gave full information as to new processes. French skilled labor was brought over. When his family came to the Brandywine they lived in a log house, probably built on the Swedish model, on the shore of the river, but soon moved to a stone house on the hill, while Victor, when he joined them in 1810, built the charming "Louviers," still standing, on a terrace beneath a forest and near the rapids of the stream.

Victor went into wool manufacture, with Pierre Bauduy, and with him imported the famous Merino ram already mentioned. But there was no profit even in good woolens, and Victor's chief service was in keeping the other two Frenchmen from quarreling, and by getting himself made a citizen and, later, elected to the Delaware legislature, thus giving this French family a native standing in their new country. For half a century, indeed, it was really a French community that settled on the Brandywine above and below Hagley falls, and largely French speaking, for the workmen who lived in little granite houses near the mills were many of them French too. It was a patriarchal industry, almost feudal, in which the proprietors worked with, and harder than, the employees. When anything went wrong the explosions were terrific, but the du Ponts took the greatest risks.

One quenched an overheated shaft by water from the creek dipped out in his top hat.

What attracted Irénée to the Brandywine was not only power and easy transportation. A further inducement was the French atmosphere of Wilmington, and French friends there to help him. Victor spoke English perfectly, but Irénée never found it easy, and Pierre Samuel could not make it a usable tongue. Some of the French in Wilmington belonged in circles familiar at home to the du Ponts. Among them was Colonel Toussard with whom Irénée had gone shooting, learning when he did so the inferiority of American powder. More important, Pierre Bauduy, who was a friend of friends at home, offered to invest $4,000 and later put in $8,000. And so the Broom power rights were bought. Irénée must have noticed that the willow, invaluable for charcoal for powder, grew on the land, and that the borders of the Brandywine and entering streams waved with it. Later, every farmer in the region was to plant willows in stream-long lines to make with their bushy tops, from which branches had been harvested, a feature of Brandywine scenery.

The high dreams of Pierre Samuel ended in a clash in which relatives, and friends of relatives (Mme. de Staël was one), tried to take over the assets of the new company. Irénée held tight to his Brandy-

wine, Bauduy was put upon a commission basis, the
others bought out, and from then on the du Ponts determined to go it alone; and control their own business. The latter they still do!

It was a curious business in organization—a
family affair, scarcely to be differentiated from the
organization of the family itself. Explosives are
tricky. They require the constant attention of com-
petent chemists and responsible supervisors. Careless
workmen or defective machinery can, and did on the
Brandywine, cost the instant death of many and a
vast destruction of property. Irénée knew what was
to be done. Along the wild banks of the Brandywine,
he built a series of little mills, each constructed like a
mortar—three thick walls of stone, a fourth of frame,
and a roof of frame—all close to the creek. Power for
these grinding mills came from a race behind, and
storehouses and finishing houses and other buildings
were placed on the hill above. Shafts were of wood.
Stopping and starting, the most dangerous parts of
the process, were controlled from without. If a nail
got under the rollers, or a bearing overheated, there
was a flash and roar that rattled windows far away,
and the inside of the mill vomited into the river or
was flung into the woods on the other bank. When a
storehouse followed, the impact was terrific. I have
felt it like a blow on the face, in Wilmington, three

miles away. Where, indeed, three Conestoga wagons once exploded by my ancestral house, spattering the neighborhood with remains of the drivers, tearing down walls, and shattering the tall clock which ticks behind me as I write.

A rigid discipline was necessary for the conduct of such an industry. This, a centralized family control helped to provide. As the new generation of du Ponts grew up, most of them were drawn into the business. It was a family partnership, of which the du Pont designated as head of the family was also head. This French family organized itself like a feudal manor, where the chief was the source of wealth and authority. The system, within family limits, was communal. No du Pont had a salary, no family in the early days had so much as a horse and buggy of its own, but used, when transportation was needed, the company stables. When money was needed (and this lasted up to the time of my early youth) the head dealt it out and charged it against profits, which were divided by scale. Everyone was responsible for the safety and financial welfare of all.

Hence, as the century progressed, not only did more and more mills and subsidiary structures line the canyon of the Brandywine, still forest covered, but a unique community of the ample houses of the powder makers spread over the hilltops and back into the country, which, on the west side particularly, became, in thousands of acres, du Pont land. The du Ponts kept their acute sense of family relationship, a French trait, but lost, as they multiplied, their cosmopolitanism. The strain of Victor, the man of the world and diplomat, died out; the strain of Irénée, the hard-working chemist and industrialist, predominated. Pierre Samuel had been an intellectual, Victor a man familiar with the best society in two continents. Soon the diplomacy, the ability to mix, essential in a business where military and naval supplies were at the first the cornerstones of success, began to be entrusted to outsiders, employed for the purpose. The courtly line of du Ponts produced an admiral, a colonel, a senator, and in this generation, a collector of Americana—but it was the scientists and economic organizers that built a small business into one of the greatest. The later du Ponts, living in their Brandywine barony, became an industrious bourgeoisie not often seen, except upon business, in the outer world. But the seclusion and concentration of this life gave it a distinction and difference. The du Ponts, who had ceased to be French, remained, nevertheless, a race apart from the Quaker-commercial town of Wilmington. It was not their wealth that caused this, although by the middle and later nineteenth century their wealth was considerable. They lived simply, talked simply, spent their money (except for occasional highfliers) on their lovely country and their many houses, comfortable rather than grand, their gardens and farm lands. And living together, homes and mills both in the country, and in the horse and carriage age, they made to a large extent their own life, which centered on the Brandywine. Du Pont children played together, and increasingly married each other. On New Year's Day, which in the French fashion they celebrated more than Christmas, each du Pont youth brought a box of candy to each du Pont girl. There was among the youngsters a lingo of family reference hard for the visiting youth from town to understand. A certain aloofness, shyness, often awkwardness in society resulted, and an extraordinary intimacy and jollity of family life among the tribe, which, in its aristocratic exclusiveness and distrust of sophistication, resembled the families of the squires in the deep country in an earlier day in England.

Behind all this was a deep devotion to a duty to be done. For the going in the powder business had not been easy. If it had not been for the wars in 1812, 1847, 1861, and 1898, the family firm might early have gone under or passed out of control. Powder making, with its casualties, is expensive; dealing with governments, precarious.

As I have said, the clan intermarried extensively,

which increased, of course, the du Pont blood on the Brandywine. Amateur eugenicists used to say that the numerous eccentrics and rather frequent suicides among the du Ponts were the results of inbreeding, like the very characteristic du Pont face. This seems doubtful. The life itself bred eccentricity, as did the life of the English squire. What unquestionably did happen in this Brandywine community was an intensification of certain traits already observable in the family. Of these tenacity and loyalty were two of the most important, which, by a familiar psychological process, often transformed into what seemed to be their opposites—idleness and disloyalty to the will of the head when the interests of the clan seemed jeopardized. The famous quarrel between Alfred and his cousin Pierre over the purchase of stock from the first big businessman of the family, Coleman, is a case in point. This well-aired dispute broke up two marriages, disrupted local society, made a cleavage in the family, involved millions of dollars, and defeated two du Ponts for the United States Senate. It was, at bottom, the result of enmity engendered by Alfred's willful love affair with a cousin, which breached the Victorian security always characteristic of du Pont marriages in their public aspects, and to the belief on Alfred's part that Pierre had been disloyal to the company and hence to the family. Alfred had his way in love, and built on the east shore of the Brandywine, near Alapocus Forest, a château, surrounded by a wall which, actually as well as symbolically, shut out the town and most of the du Ponts. With its extensive gardens and carillon tower, it is now a home for the aged of Delaware. Pierre was vindicated by the courts, and by his personal history.

This is the family aspect of the curious history of an industrial dynasty. The economic story of that dynasty, still in control of one of the great industrial empires of the world which is expanding even in this time of capitalist hesitation, has been written in detail elsewhere. My concern is with the Brandywine, and on the Brandywine, since 1921, no powder has been made, nor is there any remnant of the old Dupont industry there except the laboratories of the company near Henry Clay, where about a thousand research workers are engaged in constant experiment. Yet, historically considered, the development of this great chemical business from gunpowder to rayon, duco, etc., etc., and from the mortarlike mills of Irénée the First, to its scores of plants all over the country, may be briefly but, I think, accurately summarized. The parallel with American business in general is interesting and carries a moral.

Up to the early 1870's, the history of the Dupont

Company was of an essential industry, laboriously built up by the devoted labor and discipline of a small group of men. It operated in what soon became a highly competitive market, and succeeded by excellence of product and aggressiveness in selling its wares—which were then exclusively explosive—to both private and government purchasers. Its rise was owing quite as much to the high competence of its management, and a concentrated control that kept it out of speculative financing, as to the sudden rush of orders that accompanied periodic wars.

But shortly after the Civil War the government began to dump its surplus powder and, as a result, price cutting in the industry reached disastrous proportions. The Dupont Company, still concentrated on the Brandywine, although they had begun the ownership of outside mills for blasting powder, met the situation by price control. Through an association with other powder companies, which began in 1872, they sailed to the leeward of what law there was and were soon able, with their associates, to set the price for powder in the United States.

A third phase came after the brief prosperity of the Spanish War of 1898, which left the managers of the business old and tired men. A new generation took charge, headed by Alfred and Pierre, and a vast and energetic cousin brought back from the West, T.

Coleman du Pont, a man of the new era of financial Titans who thought in terms of millions of dollars instead of in the products and management of a mill. These men bought control of the company on a note and stock distribution basis and, with Coleman in charge, carried price fixing to its logical conclusion in monopoly. Rivals were smashed by price cutting and then bought out, alliances were made, and, by 1914, when the great war began, the Dupont Company was in effect an American monopoly, and a very efficient one.

The fourth phase followed upon the enormous profits from the European war, in which smokeless powder, most of it made across the Delaware from the mouth of the Brandywine, was sold to the Allies in incredible quantities, at $1 a pound. At the end of the war the Dupont Company was still a monopoly, had paid 458 per cent dividends in four years on its common stock, once regarded as of little value, and had a surplus of $90 million to which could be added, for possible investment purposes, the many, many millions of the twenty-odd men, most of them du Ponts, who owned a majority of the stock. The powder barony on the Brandywine had become one of the wealthiest communities in the world.

Monopoly having been achieved, this fourth phase was expansion. The plant and capital far transcended the powder business, and, indeed, mere powder was as outdated in the scheme of chemical production as the water wheels that had turned the old mills. With adroit financial management, and a recruiting of first-rate scientific and executive brains wherever obtainable, the company began the development of a vast chemical industry, much helped at first by the acquiring of German patent rights after the war. For investment, they chose General Motors, the largest unit of the new motor industry, and soon gained control. Hence, the firm that began with black powder in the Brandywine, by the 1940's became master maker and distributor of so many products that only an expert knows when his morning purchase contributes to the income of the du Ponts.

Finally, by means of industrial research, the now vast corporation proceeded to cut down the costs of manufacture. It was such work that brought cellophane into the familiar life of every household. Financially considered, the Dupont Company, since 1902, has been as much an attempt to monopolize the profits from needful industries as were the operations of any sycophantic courtier successful in begging a monopoly in leather or spices or imported cloth from the court of Queen Elizabeth. But this modern monopoly has realized that the public, and labor, must profit also if the monopoly is to endure. Both, measurably, have done so. The colossus has been, on the whole and so far, a beneficent tyrant. It has given the public more and better for their money.

The results of the accumulation of so much wealth in so few hands still, however, await an accounting. Nor can a native of the Brandywine forget or forgive the demoralization of a quiet and useful society by the mania of speculation, with subsequent collapse, which accompanied the release of a golden stream of war profits in its very midst. But the company can scarcely be charged with that misfortune.

The du Pont barony continues to spread beyond the lower Brandywine to the famous Longwood Gardens, with their glass palace, their ancient azaleas, their organ music, to plantations in the South, estates in the North, and up the focal river itself beyond the Pennsylvania line.

The Brandywine itself the du Ponts, with characteristic good taste in the aesthetics of outdoors, have kept inviolate. The du Pont country is as rural and as lovely as in the nineteenth century. As for the wild canyon where the Hagley and Eleutherean mills once rumbled, it has gone back to nature. The lands on which the mills operated have been divided among the families. If, leaving Christ Church on the hilltop, you follow lanes down toward the river, past old houses, some ruined, you will find and, if fortunate,

pass the heavy mill gates to Hagley Yard. It is silent
and peaceful there now. A grassy walk, deep shaded,
makes a graceful curving allée between full-running
race and roaring river below. On the left, the steep
hill is heavily forested, and wild, except for sheets of
bulbs and flowering shrubs planted for spring. On the
right are the ruined mills, vine covered, desolate with
fallen shafts and wheels and rotted roofs within. They
are in clusters of two, like ruined towers on an Austrian pass. Their truncated walls look down through
a wilderness slope to the hurrying river. Other ruins
of weathered stone are on the hillside, and, at the end
of the walk, the long slide of Hagley dam. It is one of
the most serene and natural parks in the world, as
quiet as a manor woods in England, as suggestive of
the past as a moldering twelfth century castle. Few
industries have died so gracefully as black powder
made by water power, or left such romantic memo-
rials of a hard-working past.

CHAPTER TEN

Quaker Country

I T seems easier to write the history of the Brandywine from its estuary to its sources, rather than in the opposite direction, possibly because I am a lower Brandywine man. In any case, if the reader will let me take the river a section at a time, moving upward for each fresh start, I will try to keep the geography from being too confusing.

What I shall call the middle Brandywine begins at Rockland at the head of the gorge and at the end of the powder region. The river crosses the great circle which bounds upper Delaware a few miles higher up, and in about twice this distance forks into the east and west branch. The west branch turns sharply westward and then northwestward, the east branch keeps northwesterly, and both cross the Great Valley of Chester County, that limestone trough already mentioned, which runs east and west toward Philadelphia and Lancaster. Here the two branches are a couple of miles apart. Above the Great Valley is what I shall call the upper Brandywines, and discuss in a later chapter. There we pass from agriculture to iron.

The settlers of the middle valley, except for a few Swedes, were English and Welsh Quakers, with a later sprinkling of Germans and Scotch-Irish. These Quakers had suffered much from persecution at home and, as a result, had developed a homogeneity which transcended racial differences. Their discipline was rigid and bound them to plain living and plain dealing in everything from sex relations to the simplicity which keeps the soul open to the inner light. It was never easy to be a Quaker, but once the code with its spiritual basis was accepted, there was a singular harmony in the life of individuals, families, and whole communities. The middle Brandywine had many such communities.

The country shows it. A rich farming region, diversified with woods and many streams, it is a land of symmetrically rounded hills, sometimes conical, curving into the side valleys of the runs tributary to the Brandywine, and dropping rather sharply to the river, which here bends in graceful loops. It is a made country, and has been so since the mid-eighteenth century, in which only an occasional "barren" of serpentine is wasteland. The forest land is of rich and heavy timber in wood lots, and occasional mile-long stretches, the nesting place of hawks. There are many lone trees of beauty and dignity, both in the water meadows of the creek and upon hills otherwise bare. No visible soil waste or hasty exploitation in this excellent valley. The friendly families came to stay, and many are still there; or their descendants have come back to build country places on the hills.

Hundreds of the old houses are, externally, very much as their builders left them, although their stone has weathered to autumn shades. These stone houses are capacious, with a chimney at each end, and an extension, of one story usually, of either stone or logs, which often was the original house. In the meadow below will be a springhouse, also of stone and usually under an oak or a sycamore, and beside, or behind, the home a vast barn whose blank walls of more hastily assembled stones are multicolored. Old silver maples, a Norway fir, a white pine, and usually a cherry, are the protecting trees. Maples shade the lane.

But what is most distinctive in the Brandywine houses, by comparison with New England or Virginia, is the way they are settled comfortably against a rising slope. There is a Quaker reticence in their placing, seldom on the road, never showily set on a height, facing usually the southern sun, and not the highway. I am aware that the sloping lands of the valley lend themselves to such a choice of sites, but I am sure that there is to be reckoned with, also, the temperament of a quiet people who had definitely sought retirement from the world. As one canoes down the middle Brandywine or drives down the little roads that follow its course, these soft old homesteads open likes coves of peace on a tranquil lake.

Industry in this middle valley was abundant but not important. Flour and corn mills still grind there, though more have been deserted, and the usual small manufactories of early industrialism once used the power. But it is not power here, but culture of the soil and the feeding of animals, that brought wealth enough to build the stone houses. Most of all, I suppose, the dairy has been the chief source of prosperity. On the Brandywine meadows particularly, herds of sleek cows munch the turf or stand knee-deep in the water. The Swedes are reported to have brought with them red cattle much superior to the English breeds and to have given to this region a superiority in stock that has remained.

Above the Forks, the two valleys narrow. On the west branch the hills swing in graceful curves, leaving a wooded slope on one side of the creek and on the other a narrow arc of meadow. Thanks to the one-track Wilmington and Northern Railway, built in the seventies to tap the lime, iron, and coal of the north for Wilmington, it used to be possible to follow this western valley almost at the streamside, and to name it by its stations, now largely derelict—Wawaset, Embreeville, Northbrook. This middle valley of the west branch ends at the industrial city of Coatesville, where power again dominates the river. The east branch has a steeper, narrower valley, often hemlock shaded, and reaches the Great Valley at Downington on what was the great Philadelphia-Lancaster turnpike over which emigrants poured west.

The capital of this middle region is West Chester, which is back from and above the Brandywine, but owes its growth as a market town to the richness of the valley. When I lived as a boy on Pocopson Creek, and drove in a farm wagon to West Chester, it was as much of a farmers' town as any place in Iowa or Kansas. One other small town has kinship and geographical relation to this part of the Brandywine, Kennett Square, to the west of the river, a Quaker stronghold where Bayard Taylor was born. Everything else below Coatesville as far as Wilmington is rural.

The historical event of the middle river was the Battle of the Brandywine, of which it was the background and also the cause. That will require a chapter of its own. But the west branch, just above the Forks, has one historical monument of real importance; and the east branch is involved in the Great Battle of West Chester, an episode worthy of Irving.

On the way down the bucolic valley of the east Brandywine from the smoke and dirt of Coatesville, one passes through East Fallowfield township where the Quaker preacher, John Salkeld, used to shout "Fire, Fire!" at his sleepy audiences, adding, "In Hell!" Below, is Newlin, where Indian Hannah lived. Here, not far from Embreeville, on the farm once belonging to John Harlands (or Harlan), is a stone, now protected, and called traditionally the Star-Gazer's Stone. This was set up in 1764 by two English surveyors of high scientific competence as a point for astronomical observation by which they could determine a boundary between Maryland and Pennsylvania. This boundary was later named for them, the Mason and Dixon's line.

The project was important, the result historical. For a century almost the boundaries of Delaware, Maryland, and Pennsylvania had been in doubt. Lord Baltimore's original grant ran to the 40th degree of latitude, which, if maintained, would have put Philadelphia and its harbor outside Penn's jurisdiction. No one, however, knew just where the 40th degree of latitude was, and, in the ensuing compromises, Penn was granted the half of the Peninsula between the Delaware and the Chesapeake which lay east of a line drawn from the latitude of "old" Cape Henlopen. This line was continued north until it met the arc of a circle drawn with a twelve-mile radius, New Castle being the center. Surveying was crude, there were abundant causes for delay, and each side fought for a decision from the British courts, finally clarifying the boundaries of what are now three states. It was not until 1750 that Lord Hardwick decreed a performance of an agreement of 1732 to run a line west, dividing Pennsylvania from Maryland, from a point on the north-and-south Peninsula line, fifteen miles south of the southernmost latitude of the City of Philadelphia. This left an 800-acre wedge between the northern arc of Delaware and the north-and-south line, which was later awarded to Delaware.

In 1763, the two English surveyors determined the exact location and latitude of the point in Philadelphia, and then moved west into Chester County and north of the Delaware arc, to set up their observatory for the final observations. They put the Star-Gazer's Stone at what they thought was a convenient location, which would save them the crossing of rivers, but had to cross the crooked Brandywine three times on their southern extension. When they had determined the exact astronomical location of the stone, they cut a "visto" eight or nine yards wide through woods and brush, ran their south line fifteen miles south, and soon established (and with great accuracy) a corner, from which the famous east-and-west boundary line could be run. This Mason and Dixon's line they carried 230 miles west until warlike Indians turned them back.

The Mason and Dixon's line divided the slave states from the free in the Civil War and became a symbol in American language. After the surveyors had completed their work, the Royal Society availed themselves of the preparations made and had measured the exact mileage of a degree of latitude, never before done on land. It proved to be 68.826 miles.

The eastern branch of the river below Downingtown and the Great Valley has a narrower, more curving, and even more picturesque course than the western branch, but runs through much the same kind of country. Downingtown was a famous resting place on the great turnpike of 1795 which did so much to open up the West. It was largely German in its settlement, and a legend, which I hope is true, records that the T's on the milestones on the Horseshoe Pike from Conestoga to this place, were carved by Pennsylvania Dutch contractors who marked each stone so many miles to P for Philadelphia, so many to T for Towningtown.

Except for more stone bridges, the east branch to an outsider would seem just another stretch of amber Brandywine water, shadowed and meadowed. Nor has anything notable happened here before and after the Battle of the Brandywine. The hemlock is common on this stream, a tree rare on the western branch or below the Forks. But in its course from the northwest, this branch comes closest to the market town of West Chester, and I will take this easy proximity—since all roads that cross the Brandywine here lead toward West Chester—to tell the story of the Battle of West Chester, a military comic.

West Chester appears first in history as a four corners on routes from Wilmington and Philadelphia, one of which was owned in 1762 by a person of the extraordinary name of Phinehas Eachus, the etymology of which defies me, who established a tavern there, called the Turk's Head. The original county seat of Chester County was Chester on the Delaware. By 1766 this had begun to be inconveniently far from the center of population and in 1784, after various attempts, a commission was given power to erect county buildings at a spot to be chosen which should not be more than a mile and a half from the Turk's Head. The moving spirit was a local autocrat and Revolutionary veteran, Colonel John Hannum, who owned land on the east branch of the Brandywine, and was supposed to desire a county seat on his own territory. His lands proved to be more than a mile and a half from the Turk's Head, so the Brandywine was left to peaceful quiet. The colonel secured land for the county, and also for himself, near the Turk's Head itself, set up an inn at what was already being called West Chester, and pushed ahead with the erection of the courthouse.

Unfortunately for the partisans of the new capital, winter intervened, which gave the aggrieved lawyers and tavernkeepers of Chester an opportunity to lobby in the legislature. In March the building act was suspended, yet there was justifiable suspicion that the Brandywine residents intended to finish their courthouse and present a fait accompli. Chester determined to act. Their leader, like West Chester's, was a soldier, but both soldiers were tavernkeepers, and, as with most wars, the cause of their conflict was economic, though the action was military. That tavernkeeping at the seat of justice could be profitable is proved by a later act of Colonel Hannum after court was actually sitting in West Chester. He built a gallery from his inn across an alleyway to the courthouse, and was opening a hole through the wall for thirsty judges, lawyers, and clients, when the county commissioners got courage enough to stop him. Major John Harper, another veteran, who had a tavern in Chester, was the Chester leader and represented the flock of aggrieved lawyers in the old capital, and his own interests.

In 1785, the courthouse at West Chester being raised but still unwindowed, the Chester contingent began preventive war. Led by Major Harper, and

armed with a field piece, a barrel of whisky, and
other munitions of war, they marched to West Chester, spent the night in the General Greene Inn, and
in the morning laid siege to the unfinished courthouse.

Colonel Hannum was prepared. He had raised a
force, armed it with muskets, grog, and rations,
stoned up the gaping windows of the courthouse,
and, like other Americans whose actions are of doubtful legality, raised an American flag above all.

Bloodshed and wall shattering by the field piece
were imminent, but both sides hesitated. Chester was
preparing assault, West Chester had been violating or
intending to violate the order of the legislature. Each
side hoped that the other would start the row and become, legally, the aggressor. For there were lawyers
in both armies. This gave an opportunity to the peace-
makers, some "pacific people" of the place, presumably the Quakers, who later built their meetinghouse near the battleground, and who hated bloodshed even more than lawyers. An armistice was agreed
upon, with a provision that greater commanders
might well consider. To the invaders from Chester
the privilege was granted of inspecting the strength
of the defenses from the inside under oath to do them
no harm, while the defenders marched out of doors
where the field piece stood. An indiscreet Chester man

pulled down the flag, and a volley from the ex-besieged fired at the ex-besiegers was with difficulty prevented by the same pacific people. However, it was agreed that the fort was too strong to take, so the Chester army came out, the field piece was turned about and fired to celebrate the truce, and all parties adjourned to the taverns. Chester had shown its dander; West Chester had demonstrated its initiative; and at the next session of the legislature there was passed "An *act* to repeal an *act* entitled an *act* to suspend an *act* of the General Assembly of this Commonwealth, entitled a supplement to an *act*, entitled an *act* to enable Wm. Clingman, Thomas Bull, etc.," which must have indicated that West Chester had won, and certainly shows that, whoever wins battles, the lawyers can always be depended upon to defeat the English language. A few years later Delaware County, with Chester as its capital, was cut off from Chester County, and all that remains now of the controversy is a contemporary ballad which deplored the plight of the Chester lawyers when the legal fount at which they fed was threatened:

> Poor Chester's mother's very sick,
>   Her breath is almost gone;
> Her children throng around her thick,
>   And bitterly do moan. . . .

Oh, may Jack Hannum quickly die,
  And die in grievous pain,
Be sent into eternity,
  That mamma may remain.

The Forks of the Brandywine, which proved to be decisive, and almost fatal, in the battle of 1777, lie about three miles down the hills from West Chester. Above them to the northwest and also on the hills is Brandywine Manor Church, a landmark for the region, but with no history except of preaching. At the Forks the west branch drops down a rapid, splits, swirls around an island, and meets the less rapid east branch in a broad stream, deepening into a long dead water bordered by rich meadows. A dam below at Lenape, now an amusement park, provides a stretch for quiet canoeing. The united river flows on through broadening meadow land into a lush valley called for reasons unknown to the local antiquarians, Dungeon's End. Its chief distinction in my memory is the vast trees islanded on these meadows, of which one tulip tree, which I have known from childhood, must have been stately even when the Indians fished these quiet reaches. Such trees are clearly remnants of an ancient forest, and indeed it is traditional that this river flat was roaming with bears; and probably it was dark and tangled enough to be called a dungeon.

The meadows continue to Chads Ford, past Pocopson Creek, with its swimming holes, past what once was Birmingham Park, a grove of ancient trees, dedicated to Sunday-school picnics, past the hills of Birmingham to the east, and the meetinghouse upon them which was to be one focal point of the Revolutionary battle; and so to Chads Ford, where a narrowing river and a transverse valley provided the other focus of the famous battle.

There is a concrete bridge here now with border railings that shut out the beauties of the stream as effectively as did the old covered bridge. As early as 1724 a bridge was petitioned for on this important route to Philadelphia. In the meantime John Chads ran a scow ferry, which had turbulent voyages in time of flood, and gave his name to the ford.

Below Chads, the river sweeps through the hills in curves below steep bluffs in the east, until it comes to the lifting rocks of Point Lookout on the Delaware line, and almost islands a lovely meadow, with an old mill still functioning, and a beautiful Brandywine house. Below were the old twin covered bridges, one over meadow, one over water, and below, again, the beginnings of the long dead water of Rockland dam, meadows to the right, a forest on the left, now a wildlife sanctuary. This charming Rockland valley is accessible only by one of the roughest roads in Delaware.

All this region from above the Forks to Point
Lookout was involved in the Battle of the Brandywine
which I shall describe in the next chapter. The home
of Ways, Harlans, Temples, Mendinhalls, Webbs,
Brintons, Taylors, Copes, Pyles, Hoopeses, Painters,
Woodwards, Buffingtons, who settled here, it is as
authentic Brandywine country as can be found.

CHAPTER ELEVEN

The Battle
of the Brandywine

LET it be admitted frankly that the adjective "historic," so often applied to the Brandywine, is to be attributed to none of the items so far recorded in this narrative but solely to the Battle of the Brandywine. There great forces met in a combat which might have been crucial, there famous men were for a day or two assembled, and of this battle the Brandywine itself was the cause. It had to be crossed. My own belief is that the milling by Brandywine water power which founded great industries is of more real historic importance than any Revolutionary battle except Yorktown. Nevertheless, in this battle the Quaker stream, for so it may be called from Rockland to the Great Valley, which roads, men, and animals were always crossing because they could not easily get up and down or around either end, made military history as dramatic, as controversial, and as conclusive as any recorded.

There are, literally, dozens of accounts of the Battle of the Brandywine, but, fortunately for one who wishes to retell the story from the point of view of the river that made it, they differ extensively under three heads: why it was fought, why it was lost by the Americans, and precisely what happened in the

losing. All accounts of battles differ in the statements
of eyewitnesses upon which they are founded. I shall
not attempt to settle the discussion as to just where
Lafayette was wounded, or enter into the argument as
to why Sullivan failed to co-ordinate with his command, or try to determine in what woods and what
defile the Virginians took their stand. These events
happened on the heights above Brandywine where, indeed, the main battle was fought. But this battle was
lost before it really began, and it was lost on the
Brandywine. Washington failed because the right per-
sons at the right time did not report the march of the
British flanking army across the Forks of the river.
The Brandywine, once Howe was on the march toward Philadelphia, made a battle to cross it inevitable,
and it was the ignorance of Washington from Virginia and Sullivan from New Hampshire of the
geography of the stream, plus erroneous information,
that caused defeat.

Germain, in charge of the war in London, had
determined to crush the rebellion of the colonies by
the end of 1777. Sir William Howe, with the main
British army, was in New York. His brother, Lord
Howe, commanding a strong British navy, lay in the
same port. Burgoyne had been sent to Canada with
orders to march down to Albany and, later, form a
junction with Howe in New York, and thus cut off

New England, where disaffection was so strong, from the rest of the colonies. It was Howe's idea to keep Washington busy in the middle colonies, while Burgoyne conquered the north. Not until too late, when he was already on his way to the Brandywine and Philadelphia, did he get a suggestion from London that he should help Burgoyne in his task of cutting a way to Albany.

Burgoyne, indeed, was overconfident. He expected to be able to help Howe in the conquest of New England, and feared no disaster. And Howe, who was three thousand miles from London, and very much his own master, had his own idea as to the ending of the rebellion. He was a big man, with heavily marked features, and fond of his pleasures, especially the women. Living in cities where there was good food and pretty ladies pleased him well. Nevertheless he was a professional soldier, quick and active when in the field, and able to plan and execute a first-rate battle. His trouble was in getting started, and in following up his successes. All the winter and spring and early summer of 1777, when he was only a hundred miles from Philadelphia, he spent in marches and countermarches and preparations in the attempt to draw Washington's army from its strategic position in New Jersey. And then, unexpectedly, he set sail in a great fleet and, after a voyage which, with detours and beatings against the wind, amounted to about a thousand miles, landed only forty miles nearer Philadelphia than his point of departure! Apparently it had taken him six months or so to make up his mind to break through to the Continental capital, and when he did go it was by one of the longest detours to gain the shortest distance in military history.

But behind his seeming vacillation was a definite policy. Howe believed in appeasement and, like many professional soldiers, preferred to use his troops as a threat rather than as cannon fodder. His theory—in which Lord Howe seems to have concurred—was that occupation one by one of the few cities in the colonies, and establishment there of impregnable forces, would slacken the none too strong will-to-fight of the Americans and lead to a negotiated peace in which independence would not be an item. He had held Boston, he held New York, and left there Clinton, with a garrison of 6,000 in command. Philadelphia, the Continental capital, the center of a region inhabited by Quaker noncombatants, and many loyalists supposed to be ready to come over, was next on the program. But he was in no hurry, and particularly did not wish to embitter a supposedly friendly countryside by marches and marauders. He should have hurried, for, by August, Burgoyne was being defeated in the north. Howe's plan, however, made long before, did not provide for aid to Burgoyne. His scheme was to hold and reduce Washington's army, and by attrition even more than by slaughter. It was a reasonable policy, but, as discerning modern historians have indicated, too slow and too expensive to meet with approval in London. How much the high-living general's fondness for comfortable cities contributed subconsciously to his policy is doubtful. It is certain that a social life, enlivened by brief periods of intense activity in the field, suited his temperament best.

So, while Burgoyne marched down from Quebec in the summer of 1777, Howe completed his plans for making his next winter headquarters in Philadelphia. Charles Francis Adams, in a brilliant critique, asserts that Philadelphia was the ruin of Howe, and came near being the ruin of Washington. It had no strategic importance, was difficult of access by the navy, and, conquered, led to no other conquests. Howe should have moved north from New York, and so guaranteed the success of Burgoyne's invasion. Or, he should have entered the Delaware in the spring, seized Wilmington, which lay below the American forts and obstructions, and then left Philadelphia ripening for capture while he moved north to help Burgoyne and seize the Hudson line.

Washington showed equal strategic unintelligence. He was bound to lose Philadelphia if fleet and army co-operated long enough, nor was it of strategic value to him. He should have been off to the north in the spring of 1777, covering the relatively short distance from his New Jersey station to Albany, should have defeated Burgoyne, and secured the Hudson. There would have been time enough to get back to Howe. Let him have Philadelphia. He could only idle there. This seems good sense, and, indeed, Washington did detach Morgan with four hundred to five hundred much-needed riflemen to help against Burgoyne. This was one cause of his weakness at Brandywine. Yet Mr. Adams, like so many military writers, neglects the political factor. It is clear from contemporary comment that Washington felt that he must defend Philadelphia and the Continental Congress seated therein. He was no Russian general, able to sacrifice a Moscow in order to save his army. He was fighting for a loose congeries of independent states ready to fall apart in disaster. The effect upon colonial morale of the loss of the capital was what he feared. He needed Philadelphia more than did Howe.

And so, at last, on July 24th, Howe set out with a great fleet of transports and guarding men-of-war, bound no one but himself and his staff knew where. But if his plan was to sail to Wilmington, or to the Chesapeake, on his way to Philadelphia, he had to

cross the Brandywine at its mouth, or on its fords, for
the upper Delaware was blocked. He sent a letter, intended to fall into Washington's hands, saying that
Boston was his objective, but this deceived no one.
Then, on July 30th, the horizon off Cape Henlopen,
at the southern tip of Delaware State, was seen to be
filled with sails. Yet the fleet did not enter the bay.
Washington had already crossed the Delaware and was
known to be in position to guard the upper waters;
and even the broader reaches near Wilmington and
New Castle were dangerous navigating for enemy
vessels of size. Small boats had not been provided.
Therefore, in a day or so the armada disappeared to
sea again—perhaps, the Americans thought, going
back to New York. Then a "forest of masts" was observed off Sinepuxent inlet to the south, but soon they
were gone and lost in the sea. The American staff
voted that they had sailed for Charleston, South Carolina, and the uncertainty was painful. Actually, Howe
was fighting contrary winds, and it was with some
relief to all concerned that, three weeks later, the fleet
sailed into Chesapeake Bay. In a few days the army
landed at the head of Elk River, only seventeen miles
from New Castle on the Delaware, only fifty from
Philadelphia.

Washington, on guard above Philadelphia, was
able to save some stores at Elkton, but to do little else

near the point of invasion. On August 24th he
marched his army through Philadelphia, giving that
uneasy capital its first sight of the Continental troops.
They were urged to keep step, given green sprigs to
wear in their caps, and, with fifes and drums, and in
spite of their hunting shirts and bare feet, made a
good impression. Marching to Wilmington, they
camped on the heights above Brandywine, prepared
to defend the old ford and the ferry by the mills. But
when Howe had disposed of his forces at Elkton, they
took a nearer position, holding the high lands of the
Red Clay Creek down to the Christina and its
marshes. There they lay, with some skirmishing, until
Howe began his march on September 8th. Somewhat
to Washington's surprise, he seemed to wish to avoid
a battle, since he was moving northwestward toward
the middle Brandywine. Fearing to be outflanked or
marched around, Washington, by a night march, hurried after him, crossing, not following as Lord Howe
said, the Lancaster road and on over the hills to Chads
Ford, where he crossed the Brandywine. There he
took a strong position to the east of the river. The
center of his army was some twelve miles above Wilmington and the mouth of the Brandywine. He had
about 11,000 men in good condition. Howe had some
18,000, British and Hessians, all in excellent trim, except for the horses which had suffered from the long

sea voyage. Washington had only a handful of mounted troops.

Howe had fifty miles to go, and two rivers to cross, the Brandywine and the Schuylkill. Washington's obvious strategy was to hold him at the Brandywine, and, if possible, defeat him there and drive him back to his ships. If he failed in this, there was still the Schuylkill on which to make another stand.

The Brandywine, from the nature of its terrain, seemed the proper place for the major battle. Its mouth at Wilmington was a bottleneck, marshes and deep water on one side, steep hills and the beginning of a gorge on the other. From Wilmington until near Chads Ford these hills increased in steepness, the valley in narrowness. The first considerable road from the Elkton region crossed the stream at Chads Ford. Below, a range of sharp bluffs, forest covered, protected the eastern side of the river. Low, open hills commanded the ford, or rather fords, for there were two, six hundred feet apart.

The difficulties for the strategist began above Chads Ford. There, for several miles the river, about 150 feet across, ran sometimes fast, sometimes slow, through rich meadowland, tree studded, and cut by channels that in the spring conveyed the floods. Hills with sharp defiles lined the easterly bank, and there were three important fords in a little over five miles.

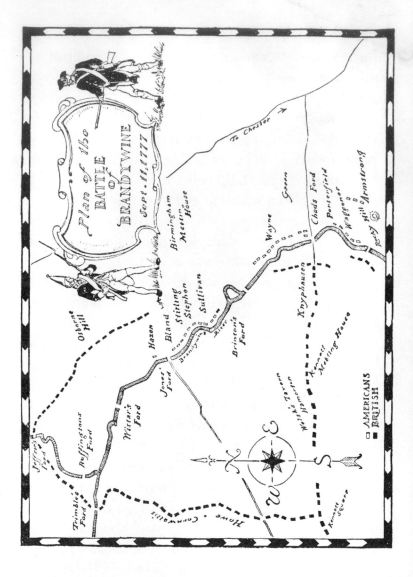

Plan of the BATTLE of BRANDYWINE Sept. 11, 1777

To Chester

Osborne Hill

Birmingham Meeting House

Hazen
Bland
Stirling
Stephen
Sullivan

Wayne

Green

Chads Ford

Proctor
Wagonor
Procter Hill Armstrong

Knyphausen

Brinton's Ford

River

Brandywine River

Jones' Ford

Wistar's Ford

Buffingtons Ford

Jeffries Ford

Trimbles Ford

Welch's Tavern

Kennett Meeting House

Howe - Cornwallis

Kennett Square

AMERICANS
BRITISH

Brinton's, a mile and a half from Chads Ford, Jones's, about another mile upstream, where the important Street road crossed at what is now Pocopson, and Shank's or Wistar's ford. Not far above Wistar's the river forks into its east and west branches, leaving a broad peninsula between. On the east branch, a very short distance above the Forks, was what was called Buffington's ford (now Shaw's bridge), the last which Washington attempted to guard. But for a better understanding of this narrative it is important to know a fact of which Washington was ignorant; that within a few miles above Buffington's there were two more fords over the *east* branch, with roads crossing them, Jefferis's and Taylor's fords. The lower of these two roads connected with a main road north and south that crossed the *west* branch at still another ford, Trimble's. The Brandywine, from Chads Ford up, was a Y tipped toward the west, the left branch of the Y still farther bent. Kennett Square, where the British lay, was to the west of the Brandywine. An army marching *north* from there could cross the west branch at a right angle a mile or so from the fork of the river, turn east and cross the east branch, and then find itself just above the Americans holding the shaft of the Y.

Unfortunately for the outcome of the battle, an informant told Washington in General Sullivan's

presence [1] that there were no other fords with available roads for twelve miles above Buffington's. As
Washington said in his letter to Sullivan (October 24,
1777), "We were led to believe by those we had reason
to think well acquainted with the Country, that no
ford above our piquets could be passed, without making a very circuitous march." Howe had better information. The notorious (and very intelligent) Tory,
Galloway, had met him and was on hand ready to
march with the troops. Either Galloway, or a Quaker
named Parker whom they commandeered as guide,
knew of the two fords across the Forks of the Brandywine, which were certainly not "circuitous," since the
route over them passed only about a mile above Buffington's where Washington placed his last outpost.

So on September 8th part of the British army left
the head of Elk, and marched up through the pleasant
Maryland country into Delaware near Hockessin;
and, by the 10th, all the army had reached the Quaker
village of Kennett Square, just north of the semicircle
that bounds Delaware on the north. Skirmishers attacked the outposts and advances, but the countryside
seemed not unfavorable to the troops, although the
information given Howe in New York, that this region was full of loyalists who would rise to join him,
was not confirmed. Actually it was a country of non-

[1] Sullivan's Papers, Nov. 9, 1777.

combatants through which he was passing. The women were frightened, the young people curious to see so great a spectacle, but most of the Quaker farmers stayed quietly at home and went about their business. They had had little experience with violence and war, and proposed neither to run away from it nor countenance it. Where the troops halted, however, crowds flocked. It was circus day before circuses, at least for the young.

Howe posted General Knyphausen and his Hessians on the hills above the fords of the Brandywine. Across the river the Americans were waiting in a defensive formation, stretching over nearly four miles, but with a heavy concentration near Chads Ford. The rough wooded heights below were held by General Armstrong with the Pennsylvania militia. No attack was expected here, and none came. The center, at Chads, was held by General Greene in reserve, and the brigades of Anthony Wayne and the two Virginians, Weedon and Muhlenberg, with Maxwell's light infantry. Captain Proctor's artillery was placed on a height above the ford. Upstream, between the meadows and the crests of the hills, Sullivan's, Stephen's, and Sterling's troops were set between Brinton's ford and Jones's. Sullivan, in his letter to Hancock of October 25th, six weeks only after the battle, says that he was not ordered to his post until the eve-

ning before the action and then immediately sent the
Delaware regiment to the first ford, one battalion of
Colonel Hazen's troops to the ford above, and another to Buffington's just beyond the Forks. He gets
the names of the fords mixed in this letter, but this
seems to have been the disposition of the guards. At
Buffington's, beyond which there was supposedly no
crossing, a Major Spear was, according to Colonel
Carrington, the historian of the battles of the Revolution, in command. The only source I can find for the
statement that he was in command is a remark by the
reliable Benjamin Lossing, on whom Carrington often
depends, to be found in his *Pictorial Field-Book of the
Revolution.* He says that Major Spear was "posted"
at Buffington's. We shall hear more of Major Spear.

But the Americans were not merely on the defensive. Early in the morning of the 11th, General
Maxwell crossed the river with what riflemen he had
been able to gather after Morgan had been sent north
to meet Burgoyne. There was sharp skirmishing near
Welch's tavern and the Kennett meetinghouse on the
lands to the east of Kennett Square. Repulsed, he retook the heights just above the river, using reinforce-
ments, and, at the same time, Porterfield and Wag-
goner from the American center crossed below him
and prepared for an assault on Knyphausen's army.
But Knyphausen was too strong for them, and, after

a column had been sent toward Brinton's ford, out-flanking Maxwell, the Americans were forced to re-cross the river. This was the beginning of the battle. It was already clear that Washington intended to take the offensive when he could. Now Knyphausen oc-cupied the westerly heights above the river, and set his batteries to play opposite Proctor's on the other side. His orders were to "amuse" the Americans, while more serious tactics were developing.

They had begun at dawn. Three miles behind Knyphausen's position, General Cornwallis, with Howe accompanying, had led off about 7,000 [1] of the British army on the north and south Great Valley road which gradually approaches the westward bend-ing Brandywine, crosses the west branch beyond the Forks, and leads, or led, eventually to Martin's tavern near Marshallton, on the road from Lancaster to Philadelphia, and then to the Great Valley nine or ten miles to the north of Chads Ford. This road Corn-wallis left in order to cross the Fords just above the American army. It was a flanking movement which General Sullivan said he expected all along, beautifully executed. Dawn came in a dense September fog, which heavily shrouded the troops as they marched, north at first, some six miles away from the nearest

[1] The numbers are variously stated. A detailed list of the troops employed may be found in *The Narrative of Lieut. Gen. Sir William Howe* (2d ed.). London, 1780.

American troops, but with no intention of keeping on as far as Martin's tavern and the crossroad to Lancaster. Cornwallis proposed to turn east at the Forks, and so outflank the Americans.

The march, in spite of the fog, was detected, but its purpose was not clear. Colonel Bland, crossing Brinton's ford on a scouting expedition, had seen an army moving north. Just before 11 A.M., Lieutenant Colonel Ross with seventy men was trailing them northward, and his Captain Simpson had fired upon them from ambush. By then Cornwallis's advance troops must have been near, or across, Trimble's ford over the westward bending west fork of the Brandywine, but Ross could not tell yet whether he was headed for the Lancaster road or the Great Valley, intending perhaps to march clear around Washington's army to Philadelphia, or proposing to cross the Forks region lower down, and so secure a dangerous flanking position just north of the American army on the east bank.

The message reached Washington before noon and determined his whole plan of battle. It was confirmed by a report of Colonel Hazen's transmitted by Major Morris to Washington, that the enemy had been seen near the Forks.

Howe seemed to be evading battle, and, indeed, Ross reported that the general himself was with the northward marching army. In any case, he was far away from Chads Ford, with what seemed, at best, a long circuit to make before he could cross the river and, if he intended to flank, come down the east bank upon the Americans. Washington resolved to attack with his whole force while the British army was thus split. He ordered Greene to cross the river to the south, perhaps at Pyle's ford below Chads, where his march would be concealed by woods until he had outflanked Knyphausen. He himself would command a frontal attack across the fords at Chads, while General Sullivan, at Brinton's above, was ordered to cross and either attack the flanking British army if it had turned toward the river below the Forks or outflank it if it was trying to cross above, or moving to the north. It was a bold and promising plan which might have led to a Napoleonic victory, by engaging, with equal or superior forces, one part of the enemy at a time.

But more news came in, and it was this fatal message that made the turning point of the battle before it had reached a climax.

General Sullivan, whose responsibility it was to watch the fords, and find and attack a flanking army, was a high-strung man, brave, patriotic, but likely to lose his head in an emergency. On August 7th, he had written to Washington that he was wrecked by fatigue, ill, and probably never would be really well again. Since then, he had undertaken an injudicious raid upon Staten Island, for which he was later tried by the Congress. His troops were weary, and, in spite of Washington's order not to fatigue them by haste, both troops and general were probably out of condition when they arrived late to support Washington. It was not his fault that he believed there were no good crossings above his picket at Buffington's; it was surely his duty to make sure. When Ross's message came toward noon, he was confirmed in his opinion that there would be a flanking movement, but completely vague as to how it might be accomplished. He was prepared, but not ready.

Then suddenly—it could scarcely have been much after noon, and possibly earlier—that same Major Spear who had been posted at Buffington's ford, appeared with contradictory information:

"General Sullivan to General Washington . . .

'Brinton's Ford, Sepr 11, 1777

Dr General Since I Sent you the message by Major Morris I saw Major Joseph Spear of the Militia who Came This morning from a Tavern Called Martins on the Forks of Brandywine—he Came from thence to Welches Tavern & heard nothing of the Enemy about the Forks of the Brandywine & is Confident they are not in that Quarter So that Col. Hazen's Information must be wrong. I have

Sent to that Quarter to know whether there is any foundation for the Report & shall give yr Exc^y the Earliest
Information.' "

He did send Sergeant Tucker on horseback, who
got as far as the Lancaster road, and reported no
enemy heard of or in sight. Yet by noon some British
must have crossed the Forks, only a mile above Buffington's, since by 1:15 Colonel Bland saw their advance guards as far down as Birmingham, three miles
below on the east bank.

Washington recognized the decisive nature of
this misinformation, for in his kindly letter of October 24th to Sullivan, whose recall from the army he
had negatived, he says, "Although I ascribed the misfortune which happened to us on the 11th of September, principally to the information of Major
Spear transmitted to me by you; yet I never blamed
you for conveying that intelligence. On the contrary,
considering from whom, and in what manner it came
to you, I should have thought you culpable in con-
cealing it. The Major's rank, reputation, and knowledge of the country gave him a full claim to credit
and attention."

This message was a turning point. Sullivan, who
afterward stated that he did not credit it, sent it on
without comment. Washington was thrown into a

most painful uncertainty. Was the march of Cornwallis only a feint? Was he returning to rejoin Knyphausen, perhaps moving undetected down the west side of the Brandywine, hoping to fall upon Washington's rear if he should be so rash as to cross the river? Or was he on his way to Philadelphia, leaving Knyphausen to fight a rear-guard action? With what must have been a quick decision, the commander in chief reversed his orders. Greene was stopped at the river's edge; the whole frontal attack across the Brandywine was called off.

And then, just before 2 P.M., in rode one "Squire Cheyney," identifiable as a Chester County patriot who, though English by birth, had been employed as a spy. The British, he said, had crossed the Forks and were on their way down. Sullivan distrusted him but sent him on to Washington, who was also doubtful. But upon his heel came Colonel Bland's report, written at 1:15, of the British advancing to the north and east of the American army. The trap was sprung. If Washington had not called off his frontal attack, his army might have been lost across the river. But Major Spear's erroneous message, and Sullivan's failure to get earlier and better information from his advance guard at Buffington's, had resulted in a surprise by a flanking force and a danger of utter defeat.

The disposition of the American army had to be

completely reorganized in the briefest time. In an hour the battle was raging desperately at the north, while Knyphausen, still at Chads Ford below, prepared to pinch the Americans between Cornwallis and himself by crossing the river and attacking their center. It must have looked to Washington like destruction.

Who was this Major Joseph Spear, to whom even Washington ascribed the misfortune of September 11th? Sullivan, in his October 6th letter to John Hancock, says that he "came to me & inform'd that he was from the upper country, that he had come in the Road, where the enemy must have passed to attack our right and that there was not the least appearance of them in that Q^r & added that Gen. Washington had sent him out for the purpose of discovering whether the enemy were in that Q^r."

It is not surprising that the historians of the battle, failing to identify him, have wondered whether he was not a British spy or, more probably, a loyalist ready to help the British army in spite of his rank in the militia. There were many such in the American army.

He was stated to be a Pennsylvanian, a militia officer, and from the upper country, presumably of the Brandywine, since it was assumed that he would know the region of the Forks. A search in the Penn-

sylvania Archives of the Revolution [1] and in documents reprinted by Futhey and Cope in their 1881
History of Chester County makes his identity quite
certain. The Pennsylvania militia had been called out
to resist Howe's invasion. Now on March 2, 1777, the
Executive Council of the state had appointed, as lieutenant of Chester County, with rank of colonel, a
highly responsible officer whose duty was to prepare
defense and command the militia until called into
active service. He organized eight battalions from the
county, of which the eighth battalion had as major
Joseph Spear, who was commissioned September 6,
1777, just five days before the battle. A Joseph Spier
(his name is spelled both ways in the militia reports)
was appointed in 1780, with other responsible citizens, to collect horses from the disaffected for the use
of the government. On May 10, 1780, in the election
of officers for the eighth battalion for the year, Joseph Spear was "chosen" again to be major, and in
1780 or 1781, but probably in April of 1781, the
dating is confused, he was made lieutenant colonel in
command of the battalion. There were other Spears
from Pennsylvania in the regular line regiment but
no Joseph. It is Joseph whom Sullivan mentions as a
major and of the militia, and who must be the man
recorded in the militia lists. It would seem probable

[1] Fifth Series, Vol. V, 801, 820, 843, Harrisburg, 1906.

that Washington, inquiring among the Pennsylvania militia officers on the day before the battle for some-one familiar with the region near the Forks, had found Joseph Spear, just commissioned from the Chester County region, detached him from his bat-talion, and sent him scouting above Buffington's. Surely his later record is not that of a man who could have been suspected as a bearer of intentionally mis-leading information or of having been a spy.

And yet, even if a responsible Pennsylvanian, commanding a militia battalion with a reputation known to Washington, Joseph Spear may seem to those who consider his story carefully to have lied to Sullivan. I do not think so. There is a perfectly pos-sible explanation of Spear's mistake, and an equally good reason why one army might march past another on a Pennsylvania morning with so little and such confused information coming through.

Spear may have slept at Martin's tavern, cer-tainly he left there early in the morning of the 11th. His natural course, which is borne out by his remarks, was to ride down the road from the Great Valley up which, at the other end, Cornwallis's men were marching in the fog. If he had continued this way and on around the corner at Kennett Square to Welch's tavern which, according to Sullivan's note, he visited after Martin's, he would, of course, have met and passed the British army. But his business was with a possible crossing of the Brandywine. Hence it was natural that a mile or so below Martin's tavern he should have taken the crossroad which then led across the Forks, the road that Howe was soon to traverse. From here, in order to get to Welch's tavern, he might have made his way to Jones's ford at Pocopson from which the Street road proceeded to Parkersville, near enough Welch's tavern to make sure that an army was still in the neighborhood. Welch's, that morning, must have been in British hands. In this way, he would have traversed, as he said he did, the roads by which the enemy would have had to come in order to flank the American army. He rode down the Valley road above the region of the Forks, while they, on the same road, were to the south of him. He crossed the Forks, which they were to cross later, before they reached them. He went on toward Kennett Square, probably on the Street road, which would have been their probable route *if* they had tried to cross the river *below* the Forks. Naturally he did not see them, although they may have been only a few miles away to the west. And hearing, when he reached Sullivan, that Ross had seen the army on the northern road, he must have said that they had either gone on north, or turned back. For they were not in the Forks, nor in the region bordering the lower fords of the Brandywine.

We can dispose of Major Spear as a presumably honest, but certainly unfortunate observer. Sullivan, however, is not so easily cleared. All he did was to send Sergeant Tucker galloping, who must have ridden due north above the Forks before noon, and back from the Lancaster road along the easterly heights before the British reached them. Sullivan did nothing more than wait for orders, and get confused when, shortly after two, they came.

But how in the name of all known military operations could a great army march all morning in an arc so near the American troops, how could it have crossed the Forks only a mile or so away from an American battalion, without some Pennsylvanian Paul Revere riding across hills and fields to warn that the Americans were about to be outflanked! For the country was well settled and, though woodier than now, open enough for observation. There was the fog, of course, in the morning but by noon that was cleared, and Joseph Townsend, soon to be quoted at length, saw the British approaching the second ford, their arms and bayonets bright as silver, for the day was "clear and excessively warm." And yet, in this army's two miles of crucial march across the Forks, which made its purpose and destination manifest, none of the many civilians who must have seen it reported it to the Americans.

To endeavor to explain, it will be necessary to leave the battle, now strategically ended, but tactically just begun, with a digression into the social and religious history of the Brandywine valley.

The rich hill and valley lands through which Howe had marched his 18,000 troops to Chads Ford, were settled with one of the largest blocks of the "peculiar people" called Quakers to be found anywhere in the world. They had, most of them, come over under William Penn's auspices, and brought with them industry and a means of livelihood. The vast manors and grants of the seventeenth century were soon broken up into prosperous farms of from one hundred to two hundred acres, and here these Friends had lived, many into a third generation, far away from wars, and with only rumors of wars from the western and northern borders. There were no Indian troubles in this favored land, except for the trifling quarrels over fishing already recorded. They were a people committed by their discipline to peace and nonaggression, and unaccustomed to violence. For nearly a century this population, so predominantly Quaker that even the non-Quakers who lived among them often adopted their plain clothing and plain speech, had lived in a quiet prosperity, in which it was not difficult to hate war.

Avarice they were sometimes accused of, but

never of violence. When the verbal disputes began between the colonies and Great Britain, they took, being
radical in principle, the American side. But when, in
1775, armed resistance was threatened, they adopted,
at their annual meeting, and in spite of the opposition
of the younger members, a strong resolution against
insurrection and the breaking of the laws. This was
held against them later; but only five months further
on, as Futhey and Cope point out, Congress issued an
address quite as loyal to the king. What the Quakers
intended to insist upon and carry into their discipline
was a strict neutrality in the practice of war and
illegality. It is possible that there were as many loyalists among them as among their worldly neighbors,
but no more. The truth is hard to get at, for the good
Friend felt it his duty to take no public stand for
either side. My own family were Wilmington
Quakers, of whom one was a friend of Washington
and definitely a Whig; but another ancestor and his
brother-in-law, who is careful in his already mentioned Journal to express no partisanship whatsoever
in a war which he felt to be wicked as such, was by
family tradition truly patriotic in his sentiments. So
strongly was this discipline felt and enforced that
honest Quakers went to Virginia for concentration
and were even shot, rather than contribute to the
fighting. In Kennett meeting, Adam Seed, only eight

days after the Battle of the Brandywine, offered a public profession of regret for having so far forgotten his principles as to make wheels for cannon carriages. And young Joseph Townsend, being caught by a Hessian captain with a flourished sword, and ordered to take down a fence, complied as far as the second rail, and then, "I was forcibly struck with the impropriety of being active in assisting to take the lives of my fellow-beings, and therefore desisted from proceeding any further in obedience to his commands."

These instances are typical. The region which Howe had been led to believe was loyalist was not in all probability, except in a small minority, in sympathy with British aims and the British invasion. It was nonbelligerent, noncombatant, and nonparticipating to a high degree. These obstinate Friends could not, consistently with their principles, take any active part in the war, and "generally," says Joseph, "believed it right to remain at their dwellings, and patiently submit to whatever suffering might be their lot." The Birmingham meeting, finding their meetinghouse commandeered for a hospital, took benches and held meeting just the same in the grove. If the young went to watch the soldiers, that was human. It was not their concern to pass on information about the war.

Now here is a real reason for the excessive failure

of Washington's intelligence. His own service was in-adequate. The population, which elsewhere would certainly have kept him informed of the progress of the enemy, simply would not meddle in the war. They had pledged themselves not to take any part, and they did not. Only such Quakers as were forced to guide armies or officers accompanied the troops. No native, except Cheyney, a spy, is reported as bringing in in-formation. And this explains, if anything can, why Howe was able to circle within a mile or so of the American pickets without detection. He must have been seen in the Forks, as he was before, but those who saw him would believe it against their discipline to carry word of the war. Joseph and some others had been watching the fords all morning. They knew what was up. Others must have been watching across the east branch. No word came. An observer in the Forks a little after Joseph Spear had ridden that way, would have seen the British army with a stream be-hind and a stream in front. They could have been at-tacked before their flanking was complete, delayed if not defeated. But the quiet Quakers stayed at home. The British army was already in Sconneltown resting on the hills above the Brandywine, while countryfolk wandered among them, when Squire Cheyney burst upon Sullivan with the news.

The next phase of the Battle of the Brandywine

is, fortunately, recorded for us by a noncombatant eyewitness for whom it seems to have been the great experience of his life. Joseph Townsend, a youth of twenty-one, whose father had a farm near Jefferis's ford, published in 1846 a simple but effective narrative of the battle as he saw it.[1] Nothing could better illustrate the professional character of eighteenth century war—a game played by strict rules between bodies of the military, while noncombatants looked on, at least until the firing began. Joseph had seen the brilliant show of Cornwallis' advance guard marching down to Jefferis's ford. This must have been before noon, since the sight interrupted the quiet of a Fifth-day morning meeting, and brought the Quakers out of the wheelwright shop which served them as an emergency meetinghouse. There was some delay in the march here, for Wilmington merchants, expecting an invasion, had sent casks of liquors to be stored, by ill luck, in Emmor Jefferis's house at the Forks, where they would surely be safe! The army refreshed itself, reportedly on madeira, but more probably on rum. "Possessed with curiosity, and fond of new things," Joseph and his brother, having run home to see whether their horses were safe, rushed out into the roads again, where they met Abel Boake's wife, Sarah,

---

[1] *History of Chester County, Pennsylvania.* By J. Smith Futhey and Gilbert Cope, pp. 74-77.

who had been among the soldiers as they marched in a half-mile arc, and said they were fine-looking fellows, "something like an army." You could visit them, she said, and sure enough, when the boys reached the near-by village of Sconneltown, where the army was resting and feeding its horses, a captain let them enter the ranks, and even a house where officers were gathered. What was Washington like? one of the officers asked Joseph's brother, who cannily replied that he "was considered a good man." "You have a hell of a fine country here," another said. General Cornwallis passed by in rich scarlet clothing, "very tall and sat very erect." The officers were "stout, portly men," their skins were as white and delicate as is customary for females brought up in large cities or towns." There was a contrast already with the scrawny, sunburn American type. Wandering through the crowd, Joseph came to the German troops, "many of them wore beards on their upper lips, which was a novelty in that part of the country." Thus the mustache first came to Chester County, which may have been what intrigued Sarah Boake. As the sightseers pushed on, a movement began in the troops. Hurrying to one side, they soon saw the whole army on the march, "a grand view, scarcely a vacant space left," in the fields.

But while they were "amusing" themselves "with this wonderful curiosity," the curiosity began to fire

and be fired upon. Joseph retired rapidly, "having ex-
ceeded the bounds of prudence." The Hessian commander aforesaid caught him on the way and set him
to fence stripping, but he escaped and, seeing a number of his acquaintances gaping at a large group on
horseback on Osborne's hill, joined them, and found
himself in the midst of the British general staff watching and controlling the battle. These were ringside
seats, indeed! There was Howe, mounted on a thin
horse, "a large portly man of coarse features," who
seemed to have lost his teeth. Joseph was near enough
to see the size of his spurs. Suddenly a roar of cannon
and volumes of smoke came from the direction of
distant Chads Ford. Knyphausen had heard the firing
of the flanking army and was setting his half of the
vise in motion! The British army below them began
to hasten. For four hours they marched past, leaving
piles of baggage and blankets in the fields. A flock of
rabble and plunderers followed them. "The whole
face of the country around appeared to be covered
and alive." It was a great show.

But, for the Americans, it was a disastrous spectacle. By the time Cheyney and Bland had persuaded
Washington that he was flanked, Cornwallis was already beginning his march down from Sconneltown.
Stephens and Sterling hurried their brigades of the
right wing up from the river to the heights by Bir-

mingham meetinghouse. Sullivan, in command, was
to take their left wing, but could not find the other
commanders, and when he came out into the open
was well to the left. In a hasty attempt to close the
gap, his men fell into confusion, and, being attacked
by the enemy, broke and were routed. He resisted
himself with his artillery, and so did Stephens and
Lord Sterling, but General De Borré, an experienced
French officer, who commanded the right, gave way
quickly. As this gentleman resigned shortly after the
battle, his failure was never investigated, but Sullivan,
in his letter to Hancock of October 17, 1777, has his
revenge upon him—"the *valorous & entrepid General
De Borre* whose Sagacity first Discovered That the
British Troops affixed Fishhooks to their Balls one of
which (as he Informed General Conway) unfortunately wounded him in the Cheek as he was Running
Away from the Enemy at Brandywine."

Sullivan, throughout this day, is a picture of a
weary, overstrained man, brave but not discerning.
He arrived at the field of battle only in time to help
with what troops he could rally in holding the enemy
back for an hour and forty minutes, and except for
the firmness of the other brigades he would have been
swept away after the rout of his men.

General Washington, near his headquarters on
the cross valley road from Chads to Philadelphia, was

apprised of what was happening, and, commandeering
an old Quaker, named Joseph Brown, set him on a
good horse and ordered him to make across country
for Birmingham. The frightened Quaker cleared
fences and hedges, with the general just behind, shouting "Push along, old man! push along, old man!" The
Virginia troops, ordered to the rescue, marched four
miles in forty minutes. These troops from the center
and reserves, with Greene and Washington commanding, took position in defiles leading toward Dilworth
on the road to Chester, and opened ranks to let Sullivan's routed men, and the withdrawing right wing,
go by. Here, by valorous resistance, the defeat was
changed into a retreat.

But it was very close to catastrophe. Cornwallis's
divisions had got between the Brandywine and Sullivan's command, which could no longer retreat upon
Chads Ford. There Knyphausen, knowing that the
flanking movement was complete, rushed the ford
with heavy loss from Proctor's batteries, smashed
Wayne's men on the other side, took the redoubts
above, and occupied the road to Philadelphia. It was
a trap, with only one way out—to the southeast toward Chester before Knyphausen could block that
road in his easterly advance, and before Cornwallis
could swing his divisions together in pursuit from the
north.

The early dusk of September came, Howe ordered a halt, for which he was afterward bitterly criticized in Parliament. Washington, marching by night, and picking up the Pennsylvania militia from below Chads as he went, made a safe and not too disorderly retreat to Chester and the river below Philadelphia. His casualties were toward a thousand, Howe's half that number. Next day Howe took Wilmington in order to care for the wounded of both armies. It was a gentleman's war. Nevertheless, he captured the president of Delaware State in his bed, and loaded a warship with papers and valuables.

And thus the fords of the Brandywine, the deficiency of the intelligence service, and the look-on-but do nothing attitude of the Brandywine Quakers, made the Battle of Brandywine into a near catastrophe. Washington, it seems, had only one chance to win, once Howe's flanking movement was planned. He could have struck him at the Forks, while Knyphausen was being held or overwhelmed at Chads Ford. But Major Spear said there were no British in the Forks, and no farmer rode in during the crucial hours between eleven and one to bring word of an enemy trying to cross both arms of the Brandywine.

Washington moved on to the defense of the Schuylkill, resting and refitting at Philadelphia and Germantown. Howe, who had failed to pursue on the

11th, lingered at Chads Ford, and when he set out for Philadelphia found the Americans in an excellent position, which was marred by the defeat of Wayne's advance guard at Paoli. The Schuylkill was crossed, and on the 27th Howe entered Philadelphia. He had captured his winter quarters. Congress fled to Lancaster, and then to York. But on October 4th, Washington counterattacked at Germantown, and, except for more fog and confusion, might have won the battle. The spirited defensive after a dangerous surprise at Brandywine had lifted the morale of his troops. But, soon after, the forts on the Delaware fell and there was no more to do except settle down for the terrible winter at Valley Forge, a hungry wolf watching Howe's fat sheep in comfortable Philadelphia only a few miles away.

Behind, at the Brandywine, in the weeks after the battle, there was wide pillaging by the soldiers and plunderers. Characteristically when, later, offer of restitution was made by the local government, the Quakers refused to list their losses. They would not be paid even for their sufferings by the wagers of war. The indefatigable Joseph saw the wreckage left behind a great battle. When the tide of fight swept beyond Birmingham meetinghouse, he proposed to some of his companions to go over the battlefield since they might never have another chance. With reluctance, some consented. They saw dead and wounded, and helped to carry unfortunates into the meetinghouse on the stripped-away doors. The insatiable youth was even about to witness the cutting off of a leg when he was warned to be away before the pickets were set. Twelve or fifteen of these sightseers set out for home, two ahead, who, talking "rather freely on the defeat of the American army" were overheard by an American scouting party under William Gibbons of upper Brandywine, were hailed and, not answering, were fired upon. Simon Kern was badly wounded, and Joseph, to put it mildly, frightened to his finger tips. Silently he raced home across country, stepping in the dark into a flock of sheep whose rout completed his own. It is questionable, in the final paragraphs of his narrative, whether he is most appalled by his own imprudence, his dangerous familiarity with the enemies of his country, or by the death, waste, and destruction in the countryside, left behind when the British moved on toward Swedes Ford, on the Schuylkill, and Chester, in the enveloping movement which took Philadelphia.

The region and its records are rich in anecdotes of the Battle of the Brandywine, the more picturesque, such as the death after a premonition of the heir of the noble Percys, demonstrably false, the homelier ones surely true. John Brinton, at Wistar's ford (the heart of the Brinton country), an "eccentric, daring little man," inclined to drink, shouted "Hurrah for George Washington," when some light British troops came scouting that way, but, when threatened, changed it to "Hurrah for King George!" —then added "Washington." He was plundered and arrested. If a Quaker, he was not so congenital a Friend as was the savior of Samuel Smith, a Maryland officer, later to be general. Separated from his regiment, and lost, he rode to the house of a Quaker, and, drawing a pistol, said he was a dead man if he did not conduct him instantly out of the enemy's lines. "What a dreadful man thou art!" cried the frightened Quaker, but saddled his horse. "Now," said Colonel Smith, "I have not entire confidence in your fidelity, but I tell you explicitly, that if you do not conduct me clear of the enemy, the moment I discover your treachery, I will blow your brains out!" The terrified farmer exclaimed, "Why, thou art the most desperate man I ever did see!" And indeed these quiet and upright noncombatants did see their peaceful order turned upside down, while the world in its violence rushed across their Brandywine fields. "Do not attack General Washington," said a visiting English Quakeress to General Knyphausen. "All the men in the other world are with him." "And all the men in this world are with me," the Hessian commander replied.

The Battle of the Brandywine, as I have said, is better described as a retreat than a defeat. Its only real "if" is the "if" of surprise. It seems doubtful whether, under the most fortunate circumstances, Washington could have done more than make Howe pay heavily for coveting Philadelphia while Burgoyne strangled in the north. If the surprise for which Major Spear was responsible had not been met with such resolution and judgment, just before it was too late, the Continental army might well have been crushed utterly, and, in spite of Burgoyne's surrender, peace have been in sight that year. But the rally at Brandywine against heavy superiority and the counterattack at Germantown gave courage to go on to Valley Forge. Then came the French alliance and the beginning of the end.

For the region, the battle marked an epoch. "For a long time old people dated nearly everything by the battle of the Brandywine,—it was the universal era of the neighborhood," wrote M. Angé, grandson of the Mendinhalls who lived on the west bank. As for Major Spear, except for the episode of the horses and his promotion, we hear no more of him. Presumably he rejoined General Armstrong and the militia, retreating with them to Chester, and probably took part in the Battle of Germantown, where they were forced "to file off" under grapeshot and ball. By the time of Valley Forge, all the Pennsylvanians, except the regulars, seem to have gone home. He was apparently not available for questioning while the correspondence about his message was going on in the autumn of 1777. He is not quoted or interviewed. Probably he was back in the "upper country," not courting publicity! His lieutenant-colonelcy, even though only in the militia, was surely not for his services on the Forks of Brandywine.

I have slid my canoe many a time around the dam near what was the upper ford at Chads. But it was not blood and cannon, or bones once rotting on the bottom of the river, that stirred my imagination. It was rather the memory of how this persistently cross-traffic river made a checkerboard for British and American generals, on which one move, badly played, nearly led to the loss of an army at a time when, probably, no immediate recovery would have been possible. For both Howe and Germain knew that the clue to victory was the destruction, by attrition or defeat, of Washington's army in the field.

CHAPTER TWELVE

Iron and Steel

JUST east of the pleasant village of Honeybrook, which lies under the Welsh Hills, is a height of land separating the sources of the two Brandywines. These sources are numerous mountain streamlets from springs high up in the range. Five springs, it is said, unite to form the east branch, but I have not counted them. At the foot of the hills this branch is already a sizable brook. The west branch draws from a wider area of hills and has a longer course to the Forks. But both, as soon as they are large enough to be called rivulets, have left the stony hills of sandstone, with their scrub oak and hickory and cedar, and look of New England, and have entered the bend-and-meadow and wooded-hill region which I call Brandywine country because it has so distinctive a character. A lover of the river notes a difference between the two valleys as the streams follow the two sides of their ellipse, cross the Great Valley, piercing its flanking hills, and swing inward toward the Forks with Brandywine Manor Church on its hill between them. It is not, however, a difference easily described for the outsider—nor important.

But there is a new factor in the history of what I shall call the upper Brandywine, meaning the two branches from their sources to the Great Valley, where they cross at Coatesville and Downington respectively. This upper Brandywine region has iron and copper in its Welsh Hills and limestone for smelting in its valley, and had once abundant forests on land not good for agriculture, out of which charcoal could be made. From the very earliest period of settlement iron was made and worked there, and the peculiar organization of industry and life by the ironmasters began on a largish scale as early as anywhere. To this development, power from the Brandywines was contributory.

The area of the Great Valley and north of it was settled by Welsh Quakers, who have left their names in the two Uwchlan townships, and then by Germans, especially in the valley, and by Scotch-Irish in Wallace, and in the Nantmeals and Honeybrook, where all the Brandywines rise. One might speak of the three Brandywines here in the north, for the east branch has a feeding stream from Nantmeal swamp called the Marsh Brandywine. The soft brown house walls of the middle Brandywine, flecked with black hornblende and sparkling with mica, are not so common here, even on the west branch. Brick buildings are more frequent, and the larger houses are later in date than downriver. We are out of political history in this region until we reach the old turnpike to the west in the valley, which once had an inn for every milestone. But in economic history, the east branch may be said to have been devoted to iron, the west branch more notably to steel.

The quartzite rock of the Welsh Hills is interrupted by dikes of trap, and near the jointures of these old lava flows are areas heavily mineralized with copper, lead, but most of all with magnetic iron. Just over the watershed beyond the east branch, French Creek, leading to the Schuylkill, has been a source of iron from the earliest eighteenth century. Its black magnetite, very rich, could be dug out from pits not over forty feet deep, and so was available to colonists with primitive tools. On the hills was wood for charcoal, and, just over the watershed, the sufficient water power of the Brandywines. The Warwick Furnace on French Creek used five to six thousand cords of wood annually, the produce of 240 acres. Rebecca Furnace, as early as 1760, was operating near the east Brandywine, getting its ore from the French Creek mines, and probably had a forge run by Brandywine power. Twaddell's Forge was operating by 1784; Mary Ann Forge on the east branch by 1785; and, between the east and west Brandywines, the Hibernia Forge, built by Samuel Downing on a tract called "Fortunate," flourished in 1792. Near the headwaters of the east branch, in the early nineteenth century, the Isabella

Furnace (great for its times) was built, and converted into a forge in 1853. Its ruins are now as picturesque as the ancient powder mills downstream. Cheap iron at the great Cornwall mine farther up in Pennsylvania, and, later, iron from the West, and (most of all) the exhaustion of the charcoal forests, brought an end to the furnaces and forges along the Brandywines.

Nevertheless, this upper region shared, though it was by no means central, in one of the most picturesque and individual of American economic and social organizations—the ironmaster's estate, with its furnace or forge, or both.

It will be noted that these forges and furnaces have names, often women's names, like southern plantations. The analogy is in many ways exact. They were estates, not mere industries, and, if inherited by women or dowered upon them, were given the names of the owners. For an ironmaster bought a region of varied resources, not a farm or lot. If he proposed to erect a furnace, he had to be near iron and limestone, and own forests for charcoal. If a forge, he had to have water power and again forests for charcoal. And, since these requirements meant usually a location back from open country and towns, he needed arable land to feed his workmen.

Hence the ironmaster, like the plantation owner,

was a capitalist who bought or controlled his thousands of acres, set up a little community, and was responsible for its welfare. A furnace was used to reduce the iron ore itself to "pigs" or "blooms" of crude iron. Once lit, a furnace ran, sometimes for months at a time, without going out. The men worked in twelve-hour shifts, with few or no holidays while the fires were burning. The fluid iron was run into troughs which made the pigs or, if there was a craftsman designer on the place, into molds from which would be lifted the beautiful fireplace-backs or stove-sides, with heraldic or other designs, often very elaborate, which are still to be found in some old houses in the region, and in many collections and museums.

This first-run iron was too impure and too weak for any use requiring great tensile strength. Hence the pigs were either reworked on the place or hauled to the nearest forge. For this, power was needed to run the great trip hammer, which banged out impurities from blooms that had already been reheated with charcoal. This toughened the iron and made it malleable, after which it could be shaped into bars for blacksmiths or plates for slitting into nails.

On a prosperous forge-plantation there would be, first of all, the "big house," always so called, which may have been a modest low and long frame building like one still standing in the Blue Ridge where my mother was born, or a more pretentious house of brick or stone. This, with its gardens, would be on a terrace or rising ground back from the stream and the belching stack of the furnace, or the monotonous pound of the forge. Nearer the work was a cluster of cabins, sometimes log, sometimes stone, for the workmen's families, who lived in a feudal dependence upon the big house. The ironmaster's wife looked after their health. Food, clothes, and such necessities had to be provided on the place, for the nearest village store might be miles away. And, indeed, although these workmen seemed to have been loyal and well treated, they seldom saw cash wages. A farm and dairy supplied many necessities if the land permitted agriculture, as it usually did. Up in the hills which overlooked the forge lived the charcoal burners, black-faced the year round, who chopped down trees and tended their domed fires of cut hardwood brushed over to prevent too rapid burning. From their remote camps the charcoal was hauled down to the forge, and they also were part of the establishment. There were teamsters, in addition, to haul in lime and ore to the furnaces or pigs to the forges.

Visit one of these old iron baronies now, such as Isabella, and you can still see the layout of an industrial manor, though usually forge and furnace are in ruins, and only the big house, become a country residence, remains.

The extent of this ironmaking on the upper Brandywine is indicated by the petition of one William Tregor of Goshen, who applied in 1799 for a license to keep a public house because the great road that led from the Forks of the Brandywine to Chester and the sea was carrying a weighty traffic of "pigg mettle" with thirsty drivers who must be satisfied.

But the life of iron on the Brandywine was short. The mercantile policy of Great Britain sharply forbade any working up of iron beyond the raw metal stage, and, although the laws were constantly evaded, expansion was difficult. Soon the available wood for charcoal in the fertile valley country was exhausted, and, a little later, the more extensive forests of the barren Welsh Hills were used up. For lack of charcoal, Rebecca Furnace was closed in 1794. It was an eighteenth century industry—at least on the east branch.

The west branch of the Brandywine runs farther from the French Creek ore deposits, and, until it reaches Coatesville in the valley, has little industrial history. It was in the wild Welsh Hills that Abe Buzzard—a name for the movies—hid after his banditries. He, or the renegade Fitzpatrick, may have suggested to Bayard Taylor his Sandy Flash, the highwayman, in *A Story of Kennett*, the best Chester County novel. At Hand's Pass, just above Coatesville, renegades of the neighborhood, having deserted from the Continental army, held up the rich and spared the poor, until they were caught and hanged. On the west branch, too, was the estate of Baron de Beelan Bertholf, presumably an Austrian, who had 700 acres and "three large two story stone dwellings under one roof," which sounds like the beginnings of a château. His wife, Lady Johanna Maria Theresa, had 100 ounces of plate, which must have opened eyes in the neighborhood of what, in the eighteenth century, was still a backwoods settlement. History records no more of this aristocratic settlement. According to Mac-Elree, the "Revolutionary Home of the Whig Association of the Unmarried Young Ladies of America" could still be seen in his day in these western hills. "In 1778, they pledged their honor 'never to give their hand in marriage to any gentleman, until he had first proved himself a patriot in promptly turning out when called to defend his country.' " This may have helped recruiting for the Pennsylvania militia.

William Gibbons lived on this branch too, in Honeybrook and Wallace where his father had absorbed the Indian town. Next to him was a tract called "Beautiful Garden." I wish I knew more of it. Gibbons was a Revolutionary colonel, presumably the

leader of the scouting party which fired on the gos-
siping Quakers after the Battle of the Brandywine.
He refused payment for sales made unless in Continental currency, a patriotism that nearly ruined
him. It was his mother who went to Lord Howe himself to recover a stolen cow, and was told that she
loved her cow better than her king, which was un-
doubtedly true. And it was William's brother James,
a noncombatant, who, tested by a group of British
officers in an inn, answered them in French, Spanish,
Latin, and Greek. "What is your profession?" asked
one of them. "I am a Chester County farmer," said
Gibbons.

But when the west branch breaks through the
sandstone hills above the valley and runs past Coatesville with abundant power, it becomes industrial, and
still remains the center of a great industrial community, one of the important steel centers of America. For the rise of Coatesville, the geography of
the Brandywine is responsible. At the beginning it
was the heavy fall of the river in this area. In 1795
a mill, called Rokeby, rolled iron into sheets and is
said to have been the earliest rolling mill in America.
This is improbable, since English statutes as early as
1750 forbade the erecting of any more American
rolling mills, and several of a date earlier than 1795
are recorded by Arthur Cecil Bining, an authority on

the subject. Yet the mill, called Brandywine, erected at Coatesville in 1816, seems to have been the first in the United States to make boiler plate.

From these small beginnings the great steel industry of Coatesville developed, and for good reasons. Water power by the mid-nineteenth century was no longer essential. However, the upper course of the Brandywine opened a route for a railroad to the rich coal and iron deposits to the north of the Welsh Hills. And the Great Valley, running transversely, became the main route of the Pennsylvania Railroad, bringing iron and coal from the West and hauling steel on a level route to Philadelphia.

The country of the ironmasters of which Joseph Hergesheimer wrote in his *The Three Black Pennys* is to the north of the Brandywines; but there are many families of ironmasters recorded south of the Welsh Hills, the Hustons and Lukens of Coatesville and the Pottses among them. Their picturesque life can be claimed for the Brandywine also. I came too late to see this forge-plantation life myself. But it was in a French Creek iron mine, carried down deep from one of those shallow pits that supplied iron for the eighteenth century Brandywine furnaces, that I had my own first experience of black, wet tunnels, and vast underground chambers with tiny lights like stars far above, where miners were working. Indeed, it was a broken shin in the dark, on a jagged rock of magnetite, that cured me of a youthful desire to be a mining engineer! And on that day I came back over the low divide to the Brandywine, in a caboose behind a string of ore cars, through the scrub woods of the Welsh Hills that had been stripped for charcoal for the old forges. Except for Coatesville, all this metallic life is dead now on the Brandywine, and the only striking memorial is the ruin of Isabella Furnace, its waterways clogged and weed grown, its moldering cupola furnace, like a Persian mosque of the twelfth century, its long walls and sleepy half-drained dam.

CHAPTER THIRTEEN

The Literature
of the Brandywine

EDGAR ALLAN POE lectured before the Wilmington Lyceum on November 24, 1843, brought there probably by his friend and occasional companion in bohemianism, Dr. John Lofland, "the Milford Bard." Walt Whitman may have rattled down in the cars from Philadelphia. But Poe, who wrote so well of the Wissahickon, probably never saw the Brandywine except from a railroad bridge, nor does it appear in Whitman's catalogues of rivers. Only one man of letters of eminence was bred on its banks, and none with a presumptive claim to lasting reputation.

Nevertheless, there is a literature of the Brandywine, which has a curious consistency. The idyllic meadows of the Chester County stream, and the rock and forest intervals of this middle river, and particularly the wild gorge above Wilmington, have caught the fancy of many writers, but nearly always with one of two results. The idyllic Brandywine has caused sentiment fairly to gush from the medium-calibered poetic mind; the tumultuous rapids and rocky bluffs of the river in its wilder passages have most unfortunately stimulated the romantic imagination of novelists, and bred hermits, Indian maidens, endangered heiresses, mysterious strangers, and fabulous adventures, usually by moonlight. The idyllic, which is sincere but mild, and the romantic, which is not too sincere and usually melodrama, are the qualities characteristic of the literature of the Brandywine.

In East Brandywine township, well up in the Forks and above Downingtown, is Corners' Ketch, the birthplace in 1822 of a once glamorous star of American art, Thomas Buchanan Read, poet, painter, and patriot. In reverse order, and restating the credentials of this Chester County boy who got to "know everybody" abroad and at home, Read was an excellent propagandist for the North in the Civil War, when he stirred martial enthusiasm by reading his patriotic poem, a painter of reputation now almost forgotten, and the author of at least two poems which seem likely to persist. How we used to declaim his "Sheridan's Ride" in school, with its refrain "And Sheridan twenty miles away!" It is, I believe, quite unhistorical, but did wonders in establishing a reputation for the northern cavalry which were so often and so decisively beaten by the Confederates. And no reader of anthologies has missed "Drifting," Read's nostalgic lyric of Italian beauty:

> My soul to-day
> Is far away,
> Sailing the Vesuvian Bay;

My wingéd boat,
A bird afloat
Swims round the purple peaks remote.

The American poet of Read's day simply had to have
purple peaks, and crags. If he could not go abroad
for them he inserted them at home, as will be seen in
later excerpts from Brandywine literature.

Read had a nice gift for rhythm, particularly
in his lyrics. But one has only to read his long pastorals, which often touch on Brandywine scenes, or
his semi-epics, to understand what I mean by saying
that the Brandywine seemed to breed sentimental
romance. Of course, it was a period in which sentiment ran easily in America except in Concord and in
Walt Whitman, and an American time when to be
imitative of the flourishing English writers was so
common as to be undetected, even by the imitators
themselves. These belligerently patriotic Americans,
such as Read and Bayard Taylor, were either un-
ashamed or, more probably, unconscious, of their
literary colonialism. In any case, the blend of sentiment with the secondhand fermented badly.

Read began with a novel, *Paul Redding, A Tale
of the Brandywine,* published in Boston in 1845 and
now a collector's item. It is a melodrama salted with
humor, which is American in so far as its inspiration

comes from Washington Irving. It is a wild tale in
the taste of the sentimental Annuals of the period,
of a repentant murderer and a wandering heir. The
novel owes nothing to the Brandywine, except a romantic central scene of wild woods and cliffs visited
at night and some pastoral description. But there is a
bit of incorporated verse which is, I think, the best
poem yet written on our river:

> Not Juniata's rocky tide
> That bursts its mountain barriers wide,
> Nor Susquehanna broad and fair,
> Nor thou, sea-drinking Delaware,
> May with that lovely stream compare
> That draws its winding silver line
> Through Chester's storied vales and hills,
> The bright, the laughing Brandywine,
> That dallies with its hundred mills.

These quotable lines, with their excellent epithets for
both the Delaware and the Brandywine, are worth all
the prose of the novel.

But romance ran away with this patriot when
he chose for the theme of what was evidently meant
as a national epic the Battle of the Brandywine, used
as the center and climax of his *The Wagoner of the
Alleghanies.*

The Battle of the Brandywine, as I have tried
to show, was a dramatic and spectacular contest, as

battles go, but it was a stern business of surprise and defense and improvised tactics, and the confusion of near demoralization. Though Lafayette, when wounded, told Washington that he was glad of it, the mood was decidedly not romantic on either side. The Americans were panicky; the British were after a "hell of a fine country." But in Read's alchemic glass the colors change to the glamours of the days of chivalry. His poem deals largely with the Tory inheritance of grandeur in "Berkeley's Hall," a Jacobean manor on the Brandywine. And his battle is keyed to all the panoplies of glorious, and medieval, war.

The reader will remember how the shrewd Hessian, General Knyphausen, knowing from the cannon fire to the north of him that Sullivan was outflanked, sent his regiments through the ford to strike at Proctor and Wayne. It was a tough crossing of infantry, but becomes in Read a knights' combat in midstream:

> Anon was heard the opening war
> Which called us to the bristling shore;
> And now the fearful scene was won
> Where deadly gun replied to gun, . . .
> While in the stream, with plunge and splash,
>   Though thrice our numbers on us poured,
> We dealt the thick foe crash for crash,
>   And strove to hold the ford.

> Now was the time you should have seen
> Bold Ringbolt with his towering mien;
> Have heard his voice, have seen his blow
>   Which drove the heavy weapon home,
> Each stroke of which unhorsed a foe,
> And sent him reeling red below.

British as well as Americans were subject to this kind of chivalric dream; but the British army at least kept it in the realm of pure fancy. Next year, at Philadelphia, the officers of the army staged a so-called Mischianza, at Mr. Wharton's country place, in honor of General Howe's retirement and departure for home. There knights tilted, if they did not use broadswords as in Read's battle, and Tory belles looked on.

In Read's fight at the ford, the "banner boy," with his sacred standard, goes down. The Stars and Stripes, according to tradition, was first unfurled on September 3rd, in a preliminary to the Brandywine battle, at Cooch's Bridge in Delaware; but by the 11th of the month the flag has acquired a "banner-boy," who is avenged by Ringbolt on the trooper who trampled him down. Ringbolt hews him "wellnigh from throat to mane":

> The hour was loud, but louder still
>   Anon the rage of battle roared
> Its wild and murderous will;

> From Jefferis down to Wistar's ford,
> From Jones to Chads the cannon poured,
> While thundered Osborne Hill.
>
> Here Sullivan in fury trooped,
> There Weedon like an eagle swooped, . . .
> And once or twice our eye descried,
> Mid clouds a moment blown aside, . . .
> The *Jove* of battle ride!
>
> And every eye new courage won
> Which gazed that hour on Washington.

In all this rhetoric, it may be said that only the last two lines have any true reference to reality.

"Sleets of lead," "sheets of flame," "hot hail" hiss and roar in "clouds of sulphur," until the day is lost. Yet, in spite of his clichés, and his loose and imitative language, Read has a narrative movement and often an idyllic charm which explain why, when read aloud, his poetry was so successful.

The earliest appearances of the Brandywine in what might be called literature are in William Cobbett's justly famous book *Rural Rides* (1830), and in James Kirke Paulding's *Koningsmarke: The Long Finn* (1823). Cobbett, after settling down to a brilliant career in politics and humanitarianism, recorded his rural journeyings through England in one of the really good travel books of English literature. His references are to the valley of the middle Brandywine, not Wilmington, and for the sake of faraway comparison only. Paulding, satirist and poet, followed the trail of his friend Irving in writing *Koningsmarke*, a burlesque novel of the Dutch, Swedes and English on the Delaware, with its best chapter an account of Indian warfare vaguely suggested by the fishing quarrels on Brandywine. An attempted rebellion among the Swedes is its historical source, but it has no historical value. Far less pointed than Irving's *Knickerbocker History*, it need scarcely be mentioned in this narrative, except for a hermit of homicidal tendencies who, characteristically, inhabits the wilds of what Paulding seems to have intended to be the lower Brandywine.

But with the publication in 1846 of *Blanche of the Brandywine; or September the Eleventh, 1777*,[1] written by the successful American novelist, George Lippard, who was born at Chester Springs near the Brandywine, we get a full-size attempt to immortalize the river in literature. And, indeed, if the melodrama could be drained out of it, there would remain a very good study of the background of the battle, and especially of the drawing into the conflict of a

---

[1] "Blanche of the Brandywine" seems to have been dramatized under that name in 1858 by J. G. Burnett. It contains, according to Richard M. Dorson (*New England Quarterly*, September, 1940), a "magnificent comic Yankee scene."

neutral population stirred by Tory insolence and British outrage.

But the melodrama, unfortunately, was Lippard's pride. "The legends of the Brandywine," he wrote to Henry Clay, in his preface, "are as immortal as the hills which overshadow her beautiful valleys." And he prepared to make them so by liberal doses of sensationalism and sentimentalism. For inventiveness of plot, variety of sensational characters, narrow escapes, intense loves, tragic renunciations, and the high issues involved, this novel is a scenario writer's dream.

Blanche comes of a family of Jacobites who have suffered in the cause of the Pretenders, and carry their romantic revenges into the battle against the British. She is a paragon of all beauty as she is seen at her devotions in her "oratory" on the Brandywine. So beautiful that the heir of the Percys has been drawn to her rustic solitude. His devotion and dark mysteries are inextricably mixed with the issues of the conflict. Fatal pacquets, mysterious strangers, a dark Northumberland who "married an Indian first" and so began the mysteries, Quakers, both honest and treacherous, midnight meetings by a rock on Brandywine with the mark of a cloven hoof, female outrage and foiled murder, make a mixture of which Charles Brockden Brown might have been proud. Lafayette,

Wayne, Washington are part of the story, and there is a secret meeting of Washington with General Howe in which he is offered a vice-regency and spurns the bribe. Never were Scott and the Gothic romances mingled in a more turbid concoction. And yet there is some good characterization, some really exciting incident, and the whole is written in flowing English with the competence of a professional.

Lippard had real ability, if bad taste. Dr. John Lofland, the "Milford Bard," Milford being a town in lower Delaware, reached a climax of Brandywine sentimentalism with far less skill. This Delaware poet and prose writer published his first book in 1848, dedicated to the ladies of Baltimore; his second, a posthumous volume, was a compliment to the ladies of Wilmington. A journalist and contributor to the Annuals, he proposed to memorialize the legends of the Brandywine, but he had even less historical conscience than Lippard. *Ono-keo-co, or the Bandit of the Brandywine* and *Manitoo, the Indian Beauty of the Brandywine, and Wild Harry of Wilmington* are pretty terrible claptrap, though they have some reality of background. His *Helen MacTrevor*, a story of the Battle of the Brandywine is no better. Manitoo, the Indian princess, pretends to drown herself in the Brandywine gorge, but reappears as a boy. It is all high-flung sentimental romance. Apparently here again, and as with Robert Louis Stevenson, a romantic and beautiful scene asked for a story equally romantic, which the author supplies. These are all brief tales, far less ambitious than Lippard's novel. As a literary aspirant, however, Dr. Lofland seems to have been not too successful financially, since he is recorded as advertising, in a local paper, to write anything from lectures to inscriptions for tombs and love letters, for from one to twenty dollars apiece!

There are several minor and some graceful poets of the Brandywine, including Mary Ann Moore, who wrote in order to divert her mind from failing eyesight, and reads just that way. And one poet, not minor, Sidney Lanier, friend of Bayard Taylor spoke in 1876, in his "Clover," of "Chester's favorable fields" where "slopes . . . most ravishingly run," and of the placid Brandywine "holding the hills and the heavens." He lived for a while near Chads Ford. James Bowen Everhart, however, deserves mention by name. His poem, "The Fox Chase," published in Philadelphia in 1874, is a lively account of a sport long followed on the Middle Brandywine, whose easy, open slopes, fences and hedges, and steep, rocky coves all favor the hunt. These upper Delaware and Chester County hunts in the time of my youth were not, however, of the pink-coated variety which Everhart describes in his poem. Hunting on the Brandywine

was a popular sport, to which farmers brought their
work horses, and mixed with such of the gentry as
could ride and afford good mounts, to make a demo-
cratic day of it. There is an excellent description of
such a hunt in the opening chapters of Bayard Taylor's *The Story of Kennett*, the best novel of the
Brandywine country. In that narrative the hunt is
won by a farmer, and there is more tough riding than
huntsman's display.

Everhart's chase sweeps down the hills toward
Dungeon Hollow, near Lenape, and is lost in those
swamp, tree-shaded meadows, "a spot secluded, wild
and weird," and ends over the hills beyond Pocopson
Creek, "by that rocky heap where Indian Hannah
used to keep, her native state." But though you can
follow the hunt easily on the map, the language describing the chase has the romantic borrowings and
imitative accent that the beauties of the Brandywine
seemed always to stimulate:

> The pack's fierce bay
> Rolls o'er the land, so wild and loud
> That glen and craggy peak,
> And hoary wood and hanging cloud
> A thousand echoes speak.

It would be unjust to omit from this survey
Reminiscences of Wilmington, in Familiar Village

Tales, Ancient and New, of Elizabeth Montgomery (1851), so often quoted in this book, for in easy sentimentalism it qualifies as typical Brandywine literature, and as an unforced and unique example of American folklore belongs in any category of original American books. Indefatigably pious, with a ravening appetite for death, disease, and broken hearts, Betsy was an articulate, if unskilled, soul, who gave her all to Wilmington, "this pretty town," which, for her, was the seat of romance and the microcosm of history. And the Brandywine, she felt, was its Garden of Eden, not devoid of appropriate snakes, both real and figurative. In a community which is described as happy, it is astonishing how many of Betsy's characters came to bad ends. If it is true that she burst into Molly Vining's burial room, without invitation, in order to see the corpse of the famous beauty, it was because death and dissolution and appropriate Scripture passages were her specialty. If she records a South Carolinian who cut his name on a rock over Brandywine, with "Departed—" left blank for the date when he should leave Wilmington, the reader is not surprised to find that he dies the next month of a violent fever, "to the great grief of his father, for he was an only son. 'But I said truly, this is a great grief, and I must bear it.'"

One much later, and equally faithful, work on

the Brandywine country, has some affiliation with
the *Reminiscences of Wilmington,* for it is agreeably
sentimental, chatty, and crowded with anecdote. Wilmer W. MacElree's two books, *Along the Western
Brandywine* and *Down the Eastern and up the Black*
[the Swamp] *Brandywine* are informal history following the river almost rod by rod, and their author,
if not always discriminating, loved every ripple in the
stream and every house on its bank. I owe much to
their records. And with this faithful description
should be listed the nostalgic poetry of John Russell
Hayes, in whose collected poems (Philadelphia,
1916) can be found more gentle Brandywine sentiment than anywhere else.

I wish I could include Charles Miner from Nor-
wich, Connecticut, as a notable Brandywine author,
but, unfortunately, his essay containing the famous
phrase "He has an axe to grind," and the story which
was its setting, had been written before he came to
live in West Chester, and edit the interesting *Village
Record* there. The great Audubon, who lived at various times not far from the river, is said to have
studied birds along the bird-haunted banks. This is
highly probable, though I have not been able to verify
the tradition. More legitimately, but in the margins
of literature, one must note Humphry Marshall, botanist, correspondent of Franklin, and self-builder of

one of the loveliest houses in Brandywine. His *Arbustum Americanum, the American Grove* of 1785, said to be the first American botanical essay (though Kalm's earlier book could be so regarded) began with his studies on the Brandywine. And, indeed, the characteristic intellectual activity of the middle Brandywine, where Marshall lived, was scientific rather than literary. There was something dampening in the Quaker air, which checked higher cerebration in both science and literature, as it discouraged higher education lest the spirit should be obscured by too much learning. Nevertheless, amateur and semiprofessional science abounded, especially in agriculture, geology, and minerology. The collecting and study of the numerous minerals of the Brandywine area was an avocation for retired farmers in my youth.

I have left until the last the one certain star, though not of the first magnitude, in the literary sky of the mid-American century, who was born and bred on the Brandywine, and came back because he loved it. Bayard Taylor, born at Kennett Square in 1825, spent his youth on the hills just above the river and just across the Delaware line. He did apprentice work on the West Chester *Village Record,* and, though he left early for a career as poet, novelist, journalist, translator of Goethe, and travel writer (one of our best), and died as our minister in Berlin, his imagination was always turning home. Indeed, his residence near Kennett Square, called "Cedarcroft," which he built from the earnings of his pen, was his pride as well as a chief cause of financial disorder.

His *The Story of Kennett* is a good novel, quiet in its telling in spite of its melodramatic plot, and with scenes such as the fox hunt already mentioned and the Quaker meeting which make it first-rate American social history. Sandy Flash, his highwayman, is at home in the Brandywine hills, and the narrative is never far from the Brandywine itself. Nevertheless, it is difficult to relate Taylor more intimately with the river. He loved its beauty, but his life was an escape from the quietism of the valley; and on his return from abroad he brought European ideas not too well assimilated, which colored his poetry of the region until it has little that is truly native. One sees this escape and return in his "Home Pastorals," where the Brandywine valley is always a background:

Life still bears the stamp of its early struggle and labor,
Still is shorn of its color by pious Quaker repression,
Still is turbid with calm, or only swift in the shallow.
Gone are the olden cheer, the tavern-dance and the fox-
    hunt. . . .
Clearly, if song is here to be found, I must seek it within
    me.

He sought it, in actuality, outside, in the East and all over Europe, and much too often in his contemporaries in England. Yet, if the reader wishes to know how life went on the middle Brandywine toward 1796, he will get a better idea from *The Story of Kennett* than from any other book I know. These are the people who tilled the fields and built the houses that give quality and character to the scenery of the Brandywine.

These fields, these very houses, though often over misleading captions, appear in superb representation in the illustrations of the greatest American illustrator of the nineteenth and early twentieth centuries, the Wilmington artist, Howard Pyle.[1] And I have always thought that in his minor masterpiece of literature, for he was a writer also, *The Merry Adventures of Robin Hood*, Sherwood Forest, which he had never seen, was really the noble groves and slopes of tulip, oak, chestnut, and ash along the hills and ravines and banks of the lower Brandywine.

[1] Nor should we forget N. C. Wyeth, who lives at Chadds Ford, and Frank Schoonover, once pupils of Pyle, who have done distinguished paintings of the Brandywine; and the former's son, Andrew Wyeth, born and bred on the Brandywine, who has illustrated this book.

CHAPTER FOURTEEN

Personal History

I HAVE mentioned several times the curiously emotional influences of the Brandywine. The tender-minded never speak of it without sentiment, and on the romantic imagination it has had the same unfortunate effect as a glass of wine upon the neurotic genius of a Poe. Yet the chief quality of its influence is healthier, and can best be described as affection. I have never known a river, except the upper Thames, to be held by those who know it well in such affectionate regard. Washington cannot have loved it, since its inconveniently numerous fords upset his strategy, and General Sullivan must have hated the sound of its name. But even the early millers, who worked all day hip-deep in cold water trying to save their races in floodtime, speak of it in their journals with a mingling of respect for its sudden bursts of excess power and a proprietary affection for its never-failing amber waters. While they built their mills like cliffs over its first tidewater pool, they kept the race-ways below their houses like water gardens. The beautiful canyon from which their power came was never stripped of its fine forest. There are trees today within the boundaries of Wilmington's Brandywine

Park that must have been once owned by inhabitants of New Sweden.

All rivers seem personal by comparison with plains, or even mountains, as I have said in the first chapter of this book. The most personal are those which fall and twist and slide from noisy rapid to quiet pool, and follow, like a living creature, the contours of the land. They change from year to year, like a man who changes his clothes or a woman who redoes her hair. When you get to know such a river well, you will note new cuts into grassy banks, new channels through meadowlands, a maple bending farther down until its branches ripple the current, a sycamore dropped into a pool, its roots parched, its arms a hiding place for fish instead of birds. And, on the banks, sun and Quaker ladies where there had been shade, or shade and beds of Brandywine bluebells where there had been sun. Therefore I make no apology for concluding this book with an interweaving of my own personal memories with what has always seemed to me the very real personality of the Brandywine.

I was born on a hill above the dams and races of the lower stream, just where Washington's army camped before they moved toward the Battle of the Brandywine. Two or three squares (as we called them then) brought me to the end of streets and to an open field, bordered by the high forest of Brandywine Park. Beyond the line of woods was a steep and stony descent to the races and the river, two hundred feet below. My first memories are of glimpses of fast-running water near which children were not allowed to go. My next is of an adventurous party of little boys and girls—we barelegged, the girls with petticoats and drawers bunched up between their legs—wading and stumbling across the rapids just above the old Colonial ford. Some fell in, some were spanked, but not I.

My next clear Brandywine memory is of age ten or eleven, in winter, when the old Barley Mill dam was frozen solid, something that seldom happened in our mild climate. To me, with my skates, scrambling down the wooded slopes, all the world seemed gathered on the ice. There were big girls with red, woolen mufflers streaming, big boys with "shinny sticks" knocking wooden blocks over the ice, grownups skating hand in hand. It was a fête. And in one corner, where the ice was smoother, a little old man, white-haired, with a velvet cap, velvet knickerbockers, and a tight-fitting jacket, was spinning and twisting in contemptuously beautiful curves while the careless throng clicked and slid around his reservation. Everyone else was laughing or shouting, but he had a look withdrawn and self-centered, as if he were actor and

critic both. It was probably the first time that I had
seen an artist at work.

It may have been that summer when I was taken
up to a farm in middle Brandywine where, for weeks
each year, I learned country life—how to plant corn,
four grains to a hill, how to make tunnels in the hay,
how to swim. For this last we were allowed a shallow
pool on the Pocopson, where the worst possible disaster was a belly scratched on the rocky bottom. In
the meadows beside the stream, we raced naked with
the calves, and painted ourselves with the yellow mud
of the valley. But soon, following older boys on a
Sunday, we came to the cool, deep-flowing Brandywine. I remember the bank, and the pool, into which
I first ventured in deep-running waters—and the
nettles which stung me as I dressed.

This initiation was a preliminary to many a
happy Saturday later in the gorge of the lower
Brandywine where, with young du Ponts and their
relatives, we had Hagley dam—its deep waters with
a sycamore overhanging for a diving place, its steep
rising forests, and its grand slope of swift-breaking
current—all a secluded playground of our own.
There, all morning, and often all afternoon, we
splashed and dove and explored the cool contributory
streams. In an old flatboat we dared the racing waters
of the dam, bringing up halfway down on a rock

with a crash that threw us all overboard; then, with a crowbar, pried our craft up the rocky wall of the race for another ride. Such sunburn! Or we waded precariously down the dam slope, looking for bass to tickle in the crevices, or slid into the great pothole, where, standing shoulder-deep, one's toes felt for nicely rounded stones.

Before this, I had become acquainted with the full length of the river on its western branch up to its retreat in the Welsh Hills. Yet this was only from a window in a car on the Wilmington and Northern, which followed the crooked stream as closely as it could. It was said that at the horseshoe curve at Granogue the two ends of a freight train passed each other so close that the fireman on the engine could hand the morning paper to a brakeman on the caboose! I felt sympathetic with the twitching tail of the train; since, as a small boy, I usually got ill as we entered the Honeybrook hills, and welcomed the sight of the broad valley of the Schuylkill on the other side of the Welsh Hills.

And once I camped, with three other boys equally ignorant of woodcraft, on the meadow below Point Lookout. We shot squirrels, chipmunks, and, I regret to say, robins, with an old muzzle-loading shotgun, which dribbled its shot or knocked us over backward according to the way in which we charged it. Yet we got some game, having brought no other food except some bread, and cooked the fragments in a lard pail until the bottom fell out and quenched our fire. We came nearest then to seeing the Brandywine as young Indians saw it—a larder and place of adventure.

But my intimate knowledge of the whole extent of the middle Brandywine came much later when, with other young men and girls, fond, like Joseph Townsend, of new things, I put a canoe on the Brandywine, at Rockland. Our first canoe house was an old stone barn, where the canoes rested on beams above a manure pile. On an early morning, the obliging farmer would haul them up to a station of the Wilmington and Northern, and by ten o'clock, we accompanying, they would be dumped off at Northbrook, well up on the west branch.

It was the beginning of a good day, to slide the green bodies of the canoes across the soft grass of spring or the slippery autumn turf, and launch them in the little river, which here ran quick and free around sharp meadow curves. At first the skill was to balance nicely as we shot under overhanging banks. But soon the real rapids began, where steering was an art. We know each by name. There was the tree rapid, in which the only solution was to shove powerfully toward a dark tunnel by the right bank where

the current had bored a way under the heavy arms
of a half-fallen maple. You aimed, you pushed, and
then flattened down in the canoe under whips and
strokings of the branches. And there was the fish-dam
rapid farther down—that very V in which the Indians used to spear their shad. Here there was only
one course, and that through the opening at the point
of the V; but twenty feet above a cross rock made
straight running impossible, even in high water. The
knowing canoeist swung right, swung left, and darted
through the middle. But often someone overturned.

The day ended with a drift at dusk down Rockland dam between high, wild woods and soft, misty
meadows; and, last, a night walk over steep Rockland
hill to the waiting trolley. A time for youth!

It was later that I discovered how much the
Brandywine had meant to maturer imaginations than
those of our canoeists. A descriptive chapter much
longer than this one could be written on what might
well be called the du Pont Brandywine, which has
been kept rural, arboriferous, and beautiful out of
love for the land and the stream. And another on the
river and woodland reservation left in trust by William Bancroft, which I have already mentioned. But
I seem always to have known that the Brandywine
was a stream to love. On Sunday afternoons, when
I was a child, my father, who was born in sound of

the old Great Falls, would take me to our family house, called "Brandywine," and it was part of the ritual to go down through the gardens to the race bank, and try to discover the ruins of the old First Dam. Or if not to "Brandywine," then to the park below our hill, and the dizzy suspension footbridge that crossed to the then wild north bank, where, later, I went birdnesting on my own. He had some story to tell me of every race, and dam, and fall.

I left the Brandywine country for New England even before my canoeing days, and my later knowledge of the river was a vacation knowledge only. Yet, though I have lived in the Connecticut hills longer than on the Brandywine, I still feel a stir of familiar content when I set foot on the meadows without boulders, see the hills without sharp New England angles, and the deep soil and high, straight hardwood groves of the Brandywine valley. Not England and Scotland are more truly dissimilar than Connecticut and Delaware.

I was translated into New England too early to write the book which, I fear, no one in our time will write about the Brandywine. Someone, someday, I hope, will supplement this history of mine with a book like White's *Selborne*, or that unassembled one of Thoreau's on Concord, to be found scattered through his Journal. In Thoreau, the rough, tough

Concord country, and the soft and languorous Concord River, both so different from the Brandywine, have been given a lifetime of observation and infinite detail. The Brandywine deserves this kind of natural history. Someone will have to spend his days and nights with nature on the river to do it, and both observer and reader will be well rewarded. My task has been both broader and briefer. I offer what can be done by one who, at least, has the river in his imagination, knows all of it a little, much of it well, and has read its records wherever he can find them.

Acknowledgments

I wish to thank the Historical Society of Delaware for access to their manuscripts and other collections. Several books by contemporary authors have been consulted so freely in the preparation of this work that I should like to make special acknowledgments here. I refer particularly to *Delaware: A Guide to the First State,* in the American Guide Series; *Wilmington, Delaware: Three Centuries Under Four Flags,* by Anna T. Lincoln; *The Dutch and the Swedes on the Delaware: 1609-64,* by Christopher Ward; *The Du Pont Dynasty,* by John K. Winkler; *Lives of Victor and Josephine Du Pont,* by B. G. Du Pont; *The Log Cabin Myth,* by Harold R. Shurtleff. While I am responsible for the facts and the interpretations of what might be called the supposed spy episode in the chapter on the Battle of the Brandywine, I have been dependent upon the authorities cited in the text and the bibliography for the facts of the preliminaries and general course of the battle. To Bernhard Knollenberg, Librarian of Yale University, I owe especial thanks for his help in my study of this battle.

A Selected Bibliography

ADAMS, CHARLES FRANCIS, *Studies Military and Diplomatic, 1775-1865*. New York, 1911.

ANDERSON, TROYER STEELE, *The Command of the Howe Brothers during the American Revolution*. New York, 1936.

BANCROFT, GEORGE, *A History of the United States*. Boston, 1834-1874.

BINING, ARTHUR CECIL, *Pennsylvania Iron Manufacture in the Eighteenth Century*. Harrisburg, Pa., 1938.

CARRINGTON, HENRY B., *Battles of the American Revolution, 1775-1781*. New York, 1876.

Chester County and Its People. Edited by W. W. Thompson. Chicago and New York, 1898.

CLARK, V. S., *History of Manufactures in the United States, 1607-1860*. Washington, 1916.

CONRAD, HENRY C., *History of the State of Delaware*. Wilmington, 1908.

Delaware: A Guide to the First State. Compiled and written by the Federal Writers' Project. New York, 1938.

DU PONT, B. G., *Lives of Victor and Josephine du Pont*. Newark, Del., 1930.

FERRIS, BENJAMIN, *A History of the Original Settlements on the Delaware, etc.* Wilmington, Del., 1846.

FISHER, SYDNEY GEORGE, *The Struggle for American Independence.* Philadelphia, 1908.

FISKE, JOHN, *The American Revolution.* Boston, 1891.

FUTHEY, J. SMITH, and COPE, GILBERT, *History of Chester County, Pennsylvania.* Philadelphia, 1881.

Geologic Atlas of the United States. Coatesville-West Chester, Wilmington-Elkton, and Honeybrook-Phoenixville Folios. Washington.

JOHNSON, AMANDUS, *The Swedish Settlements on the Delaware, etc.* New York, 1911.

Letters and Papers of Major-General John Sullivan, Continental Army. Edited by Otis G. Hammond. Concord, N. H., 1930.

Letters of Members of the Continental Congress. Edited by Edmund C. Burnett. Washington, 1923.

LINCOLN, ANNA T., *Wilmington, Delaware: Three Centuries under Four Flags.* Rutland, Vt., 1937.

LINDESTRÖM, PETER MÖRTENSSON, *Geographica Americae, with an Account of the Delaware Indians, etc.* Translated and edited by Amandus Johnson. Philadelphia, 1925.

LOSSING, BENSON J., *Pictorial Field-Book of the Revolution.* New York, 1851-1852.

MACELREE, WILMER W., *Along the Western Brandywine.* West Chester, Pa., 1912 (2d ed.).

——— *Down the Eastern and up the Black Brandywine.* West Chester, Pa., 1912 (2d ed.).

MONTGOMERY, ELIZABETH, *Reminiscences of Wilmington in Familiar Village Tales, Ancient and New*. Philadelphia, 1851.

Narrative of Lieut. Gen. Sir William Howe, The, etc. London, 1780 (2d ed.).

Papers of the Historical Society of Pennsylvania, Relative to the Battle of Brandywine. Bulletin of the Historical Society, Vol. I, No. 8. Philadelphia, 1846.

Peter Kalm's Travels in North America. The English Version of 1770. Revised and edited by Adolph B. Benson. New York, 1937.

PRESTON, JOHN HYDE, *A Gentleman Rebel; the Exploits of Anthony Wayne*. New York, 1930. Note bibliography for Mary Vining.

SCHARF, J. THOMAS, *History of Delaware: 1609-1888*. Philadelphia, 1888.

SHURTLEFF, HAROLD R., *The Log Cabin Myth*. Edited, with an Introduction, by Samuel Eliot Morison. Cambridge, 1939.

TREVELYAN, GEORGE OTTO, *The American Revolution*. New York, 1939.

WARD, CHRISTOPHER, *The Dutch and Swedes on the Delaware, 1609-64*. Philadelphia, 1930.

WINKLER, JOHN K., *The Du Pont Dynasty*. New York, 1935.

WINTERBOTHAM, B. W., *An Historical, Geographical, Commercial, and Philosophic View of the American United States, etc.* London, 1795.

Writings of George Washington, The. Edited by Worthington Chauncey Ford. New York, 1889-1893.

Index

273